# FALLING INTO HIS GRACE

## THE POWER OF A LIFE LAID DOWN

### REBECCA PETRIE

gabriella
PRESS

www.gabriellapress.com

*Life is a journey. A journey is one step after another.*

The beauty of journeying is that each step
makes way for the next.

*As we live our lives to serve Jesus, the steps of yesterday*
*prepared us for today*
*and today's steps prepare us for tomorrow.*

Each of us is on a journey,
the special way that Father has prepared for us to walk.

*This is the story of my journey.*

Thank you for your encouragement by the purchase of this book. Despite the challenges of being a quadriplegic, Rebecca along with Paul, continue efforts to facilitate gatherings around Jesus in countries across Europe and Asia. All proceeds from the sale of this book will go to their continuing work, as well as medical care for Rebecca.

If you would like to make an additional gift, U.S. tax-deductible contributions on the Petrie's behalf can be made to IOM, P.O. Box 2140, McComb, MS 39649; in Europe, contributions can be made via bank transfer as follows:

Name of account: Anet
Country: Belgium
Bank Code: GEBABEBB
IBAN (paper): BE49 0014 2898 2071
IBAN (electronic): BE49001428982071
Comment: Rebecca Petrie

# FALLING INTO HIS GRACE
*The Power of A Life Laid Down*

## For more information
**Web:** **www.rebeccasjourney.com**
**www.gabriellapress.com**
**Email:** **info@rebeccasjourney.com**

Design: Steven Tyrrell / www.tyrrellcreative.com

*I would like to dedicate this book to my beloved husband,*
*Paul,*
*for his constant help and encouragement*
*along our way together.*

*To my children:*
*Matthew, Susannah, Phillip, and Stephen,*
*and each of their dear families.*

*I want to thank many of you who have contributed*
*and added to my journey.*

*I think particularly of those*
*who have helped make this book possible:*
*Bill and Dorothy Leal, Steve Tyrrell, Mike Shirley,*
*Rachel Adams, Bill Hightower, Phillip Petrie, Sue Postle*

Paul and Rebecca are personally familiar with what it means for life to not turn out as expected. They are also experientially acquainted with the reality of God using "all things" for His higher purposes. These pages are filled with beautiful fruit emerging from a painful event that circumstances have used to draw them into a closer relationship of intimacy with God as a Father. The reader will be rewarded with previously undiscovered gems from their journey. It is rare to find a book with such depth, yet each event and lesson is so open and transparent. My promise is that it will make you laugh and cry. An unusual team, consisting of a dear wife and her supportive husband, will challenge your perceptions of Who God is, encouraging you to a new and deeper relationship with the Father.

— *Bob Mumford*
LifeChangers

In the midst of difficulties and tragedies the Lord is constantly working to draw us to Himself" (from the Introduction). This has been Paul and Rebecca's continuing testimony since the accident in 2001 that left Rebecca paralyzed. How remarkably the Lord has been with this couple! Whether we visited Rebecca in the ICU, the rehab hospital or back at home, we have sensed the Lord's Presence in an almost tangible way!

— *John and Wendy Beckett*
Beckett Corporation

During a time of great shock, after our eldest daughter was seriously injured in a car crash, the Lord gave us these words "Don't ask 'Why?', ask 'What for?'" We were being asked to focus not on the terrible present, but on the good purpose that would come out of it—and we have indeed seen some truly amazing things. It speaks volumes for Rebecca's close walk with her Lord that in an even more catastrophic time, when being asked to "endure the unendurable", as she puts it, she could hear His voice saying some astounding words to her spirit, "It's about my love!"

Our minds might rebel at the thought that allowing a dear daughter to experience so much pain and loss was an expression of God's love. Yet as you read Paul and Rebecca's account of their experience over these years since her accident, you will be impacted by their rich experience of love—God's love to them (and theirs for Him), their own love for each other and their family, the love expressed by their careers and supporters, and indeed the love evoked in total strangers who have encountered them in the course of their journey.

We highly recommend this book. *Falling into His Grace* is a wonderful title and the treasures it contains will enrich your life. While we do not ever get complete answers to the "Why?" of human suffering, Rebecca and Paul can help us to see plenty of answers to the "What for?" of God's purpose in allowing it. Their lives have been a constant challenge and inspiration to those of us who have followed "Rebecca's Journey'" in prayer—and we are confident you will find the same through this book.

— *Christine Paterson*
Chinese Church Support Ministries

# *Foreward*

IT IS CUSTOMARY FOR A FOREWORD TO BE WRITTEN by an honored friend or a person particularly learned in the subject matter of the book.

In this instance Rebecca tells me that I am both of these. I am her husband, Paul, and it is my unique joy to prepare you to read this book.

I've known Rebecca since she was 19 years old. I saw her first after a church service. People had gone forward for prayer. I was seated on the front row. Those who had been sitting next to me had already left the service, leaving the row to my left open. I glanced in that direction and saw a dream: Rebecca, whom I had not yet met, seated, head raised and eyes closed in prayer, radiant and beautiful. I knew at that first sight that I would marry her. (It took me a while to convince her, however!)

After the service I introduced myself to her and walked her back to the dorm. We were married two and a half years later.

The story of Rebecca's walk with God dates back to her high school years, when the pastor at their Methodist church introduced her to Jesus. By the time she arrived at university she was already deeply committed to Jesus, and hungry to know Him better.

During our university years she was constantly involved in leadership, as she had been in high school: editor of the newspaper, president of the senior class, dating the captain of the football team... She had the inner core and the charisma that people always respected.

That has remained true through all her life. She was a speech and drama major at university, and afterward taught English in an inner-city middle-school. That was only for a year however, as by then our broader destiny was unfolding. But that is for another story.

Through the years Rebecca, in addition to being a most remarkable wife and mother—and my dearest friend—traveled widely in North America, as well as Asia, Europe, and often in Africa. She spoke at conferences to hundreds, and sometimes thousands, of people.

One of Rebecca's core characteristics has always been a deep subordination to Jesus and a commitment to implement His ways in her life: in her thoughts as well as in her actions, in her attitudes and motivations as well as in her service. She has a wonderful, winsome way of communicating this to others.

One could ask why Rebecca had this accident and has suffered and lost so much. She and I both choose to look through a different optic! How remarkably she has been prepared through her faithfulness to Him to bear suffering with faith and grace, and to be a channel for that grace to others, especially those dealing with loss and pain.

Rebecca's mother used to say that if old people are grouchy, it didn't just happen. They'd spent their whole lives getting that way. True! What we are today is a result of our choices and training throughout our lives. Rebecca has spent the majority of her life in the pursuit of knowing and following Jesus. Her godliness today is the product of years of walking with Him.

Rebecca is a remarkable woman, who serves the most remarkable Lord. It is principally His life in hers that has enabled her to stay in peace through dreadful loss, and to find joy in life in the midst of severe limitation.

*Falling into His Grace* is a spiritual adventure. In it God's love and faithfulness are revealed. Rebecca challenges us to grace, peace, faithfulness, knowing God in suffering... one of His words to her shortly after the accident was, "It's about My love." At the time it made no sense to me. But in the interim I've come to see that it is about His love for those who are in loss, pain, confusion. And Rebecca is a lens through which His love can be seen. It is a lens through which we can all know Him better. It's about His love—for us!

I suspect that you will be touched by Rebecca's story, her heroism and faith. I know she prays that above all you'll be touched by the One she serves, and His amazing grace!

—Paul Petrie
Genval, Belgium

# TIMELINE OF EVENTS

The following dates provide a context for the events of this journey. There were short trips to the hospital that are not recorded here, but may be mentioned in the telling of the story.

October 4, 2001:

Falling into His Grace


October 4, 2001—March 27, 2002:

ICU and the Hospital


March 18, 2002

Trachea removed!


March 27, 2002—April 11, 2003:

Pellenberg Rehabilitation Center


July 11, 2002—August 2, 2002:

The London Surgeries, which took place during the time in rehab


April 11, 2003—Present:

At Home in Genval, Belgium


December 14, 2003:

A New Room and Garden

# Contents

# *Introduction*

MY OWN JOURNEY BEGAN IN A SMALL TOWN IN western Pennsylvania. My father died when I was five, and I was raised, along with my four older sisters, by a godly mother. I became a follower of Jesus during my teenage years. After graduating from high school I attended Asbury College where I met my future husband, Paul. We were married in 1966 during our senior year and began to work in ministry together.

Paul was involved as a church planter in North America where we were living at the time, as well as traveling extensively in Africa and Europe. In 1973 we moved to Germany where our first son, Matt, was born. Susannah was born in 1976, and Phillip in 1983. In 1986, when our fourth child, Stephen, was six weeks old, we moved to Brussels, Belgium.

Through the years I had spoken often at conferences and retreats and was much involved in training young women. Paul and I looked forward to the days when, after our children were grown, we would have years ahead to work and travel together.

Our journeys, however, often take unexpected, and sometimes painful, turns. This happened for me on October 4, 2001, when I fell down the stairs in our home, breaking my neck. The next 5 months were spent in the hospital in intensive care. The following 14 months were spent in a rehabilitation hospital. I was now a quadriplegic. The shock of change and loss can seem unbearable. It certainly did for me. But all the steps that have gone before somehow prepare us and make us able to go on.

In the midst of difficulties and tragedies the Lord is constantly working to draw us to Himself. A great crisis can become the first step in a new life and a great adventure. At 56 years old the accident had left me paralyzed. Some would have considered my life to be over. But the Lord has taken this devastating event and used it for good.

Change and loss are not usually a choice. But how we face the unexpected events, and what we allow the Lord to do with them, will determine the quality of our lives! The Bible says that the Lord is always working for our good. Sometimes we must redefine what "good" is. Often these crises become the springboard for a deeper relationship with the Father.

This book is a result of my new life. When I fell, my husband Paul, in shock and pain, sent emails to a group of friends, asking them to pray with us. We had lived and worked in Brussels, Belgium, for 16 years, but our friends were scattered around the world. These friends wrote to their friends, who contacted their churches and friends. Thus began a network of prayer that went around the world. After I returned home, 18 months later, to a new life and a new handicap-accessible room, I continued what Paul had begun, and now dictate a monthly email, "Rebecca's Journey" (see **www.rebeccasjourney.com**).

This book is a compilation from the last seven years, written here in a thematic form. It is far more than just my journey. It is the story of my husband's journey. It is also the story of our four children as well as a multitude of dear friends who have stood with us and helped us through the years since my accident.

I pray that through this story and these thoughts, the Lord will bring new hope, and perhaps a new beginning, to others on a journey! May you know that in every circumstance, however grave, God is working to draw us to Himself. The goal of life is to know Him. So now from these emails and my own reflections, I give you my book—*Falling into His Grace*.

"*For I know the thoughts that I think toward you, says the Lord, thoughts of peace and not of evil, to give you a future and a hope.*"

*Jeremiah 29:11 (NKJV)*

Note: In this compilation of Paul and Rebecca's reflections, Paul's are dated from the accident. As Rebecca was able to dictate, her reflections are dated as well. For the sake of clarity, there have been some adjustments in the wording. The reflections are not in sequential order, but are arranged according to topic.

CHAPTER ONE

# The Day That Changed Our Lives

"GOOD MORNING, DARLING..." THE HOUSE FELT COOL as I drew my robe around me and kissed Paul lightly. The tea kettle began to boil and I poured the bubbling water into the two waiting porcelain tea pots. Paul smiled, "Thank you, Baby!"

It was 5:30 a.m., October 4, 2001, and the kitchen around us was orderly and as crisp as the autumn air. The dishes were all put away and I had cleaned the floor the night before so it was sparkling and fresh.

I love October! The month begins with the furnace not yet running, the morning house slightly chilled, and green leaves still on the garden trees. The same month ends with the hum of the furnace, the house toasty warm, and the trees outside wearing autumn splendor. It was just such a crisp autumn morning and Paul and I were beginning a typical day. Being "morning people," we awakened early before the children. After preparing our pots of tea together we went to our separate, special corners of the house where we each had an hour with the Lord for Scripture reading and prayer. Through the years we had learned that the only satisfactory preparation for a busy day was to start it with Him.

My life was indeed full. Many times I complained to the Lord that it was TOO busy. Paul and I have been blessed with four beautiful, bright, and active children. Once while speaking to a group of women, I said, "I have chosen to stay at home and take care of my children instead of a career." Paul heard me saying that and laughed, "You've taken wonderful care of our children, but you've hardly stayed at home and not had a career."

Although my university training was in drama and English, my "career" had always been people. Years ago the Lord had said to us that He is a People Person. The New Testament is about relationships. Jesus' words were mainly words of love and life together. So Paul and I have spent our lives building relationships and loving those whom God had given us.

Our relational network spanned continents and filled our days with streams of meetings and dinners and coffees and late night phone calls. Not only was I involved in extensive listening and counseling, but also speaking to and leading groups of women. God had helped me, amid the press, to keep the priority of my husband and children.

*That morning, I had been reading Ephesians chapter two in THE MESSAGE translation. "Now God has us where he wants us...to shower grace and kindness upon us..."*

That October morning, I was again leading a small group of women in a time of prayer and sharing in our sitting room. Earlier that day I had been reading Ephesians chapter two in The Message translation. "Now He has you where He wants you—where He can shower you with kindness and grace." I shared this with the women and we were all happy to consider God's goodness.

While the ladies were still together I cleared the teacups and plates, and began carrying the tray of dishes down the stairs to the kitchen. Was it the fifth step or the tenth? Did I faint? Questions unanswered! I fell, evidently making no attempt to catch myself. Paul was working in his office on the floor above. On hearing the crash, he and the women ran to find me at the bottom of the stairs. I had no pulse and was not breathing.

> *On hearing the crash, Paul and the women ran to find me at the bottom of the stairs. I had no pulse and was not breathing.*

The lady who cleans our house one morning a week was working that day. She was a nursing student and immediately began to do CPR. She directed Paul to do mouth-to-mouth resuscitation while one of the women called for the ambulance.

The ambulance arrived and rushed me to the emergency room. I had broken my neck at the second vertebrae and was paralyzed. I was placed on a respirator. The prognosis was bleak. The doctors told Paul that if I survived I would probably be on a respirator for the rest of my life.

I was aware of what was going on around me, but it all felt surrealistic. The Lord seemed far away. Still, into the haze He said over and over, "It is about My love."

My journey had taken a step that I had never imagined. Had the steps before prepared me? I found myself trapped in the prison of my own body, able only to blink my eyes. Paul said later, as he stood beside me, that he could see the fear in my eyes. The steps of his journey had prepared him as well for this turn as he found himself beside his paralyzed wife, helpless and crying out to the Lord. At that point my only link to reality was Paul and the pain. Yet something within me clung to the One I somehow knew loved me and was faithful.

Paul immediately contacted the children and they came: Susannah from university in the States, Matthew from Germany where he was stationed in the military, and Phillip and Stephen from their schools here in Belgium. Later Susannah would tell me about that flight from the United States. Her mind was in shock and she kept saying to herself, "This can't be reality."

Dear Phillip and Stephen! Phillip was a junior in high school and Stephen was in eighth grade. "How could this happen to our mother when she's committed her life to You, God?" That was their question. Yet in the turmoil, each one of them held steady, stood with us, and maintained their faith that God would help us. We had together begun a new journey, one we had not planned for, but one that would eventually reflect God's faithfulness and goodness.

Many others have also walked with me through the ever-changing seasons of this journey. And so, perhaps it would be better to say "our journey." I invite you now to join me as together we consider the LESSONS of the Lord's love revealed in pain and loss.

*"For our light affliction, which is but for a moment, is working for us a far more exceeding and eternal weight of glory, while we do not look at the things which are seen, but at the things which are not seen. For the things which are seen are temporary, but the things which are not seen are eternal."*

2 Corinthians 4:17-18 (NKJV)

## Paul's First Email

From: Paul Petrie
Sent: Thursday, October 04, 2001 4:47 PM
Subject: Urgent—Rebecca

Dear Friends,

I just returned from the hospital where Rebecca is in intensive care. I wanted to get this note out right away and ask for your prayers.

This morning Rebecca had a serious accident, in which she broke her neck at the 2nd vertebra. The doctors have said it is a very serious break. At present she has no feeling or movement. She is able only to blink her eyes.

She was in distress this evening, having great difficulty breathing even with the respirator. She vomited.

Matthew arrived several hours ago. Susannah arrives tomorrow morning. Stephanie, Matthew's wife, arrives tomorrow afternoon.

The doctors say that surgery will be necessary, but at the moment the situation is too delicate for that. They are watching her closely and reevaluating regularly.

I'll be back with further information as we have it. Thanks for standing with us. We need your help in prayer.

In Him,

Paul

P.S. For those who wish a little more detail: Rebecca had a women's prayer meeting here this morning, and was going down the stairs with a tray in her hands. It seems she lost consciousness and fell. When I got there her head was bent back badly, she had stopped breathing and had no pulse. Thankfully, the lady who cleans our house one morning a week was here. She is studying nursing. She immediately began CPR and instructed me to start mouth-to-mouth resuscitation. I believed this saved her life. The Emergency team arrived in about ten minutes—ten very long minutes. She didn't regain consciousness until after she arrived at the hospital. �֎

CHAPTER TWO

# Suffering...Lessons of Love

"*Therefore we do not lose heart. Though outwardly we are wasting away, yet inwardly we are being renewed day by day. For our light and momentary troubles are achieving for us an eternal glory that far outweighs them all. So we fix our eyes not on what is seen, but on what is unseen. For what is seen is temporary, but what is unseen is eternal.*"

2 Corinthians 4:16-18 (NIV)

"*I now rejoice in my sufferings for you, and fill up in my flesh, what is lacking in the afflictions of Christ, for the sake of His body, which is the church...*"

*Colossians 1:24 (NKJV)*

SUFFERING IS ONE EXAMPLE OF HOW THE PAST prepares us to cope with the present. Twenty years ago I was a young mother and my life was full. I was walking in the strong reality of companionship with the Lord and teaching women at home and across the country. While preparing for a women's conference with about 500 participants, I felt the Lord say, "Teach them about suffering." Interesting subject! But not exactly what they, or I, had expected. Suffering was fresh to me then. We had just walked through a painful time when our oldest son had been diagnosed with a serious disease. For Paul and me, our deepest ache had always been when God had allowed our children to be touched. I remember Paul crying out, "Lord, please let it be me, and not him." When our son left for school, a happy 10 year old, we never knew if he would come home walking with his lunchbox in hand, or be carried in after having become ill at school. I can't even write about it now without feeling the pain of those days. I didn't know then that God would heal him some years later, and that his life would be healthy, and oh, so productive and full.

During those days, through the pain, something was changing in my soul! God was enlarging me and, in my desperation, I found the Father even more deeply. What was not yet clear to me was that those were days of preparation, preparing me to find joy in the suffering that was to come. In this chapter we will look at the way the Father enlarges our souls, giving us new capacity for Himself and for what He's calling us to, in the midst of suffering.

## DURING ICU AND THE HOSPITAL

Immediately after the accident, October 4, 2001 – March 27, 2002

### ❀ It is About My Love

The days after the accident were a blur. I was disoriented. What had happened and where was I? What was this terrible pain? I was heavily drugged and thus this swirling sense of unreality. Even so, a few things were real: my beloved, Paul and our children were close by.

*"O Lord, why have You left me? Where are you?"*
*I longed for the sense of His presence, but God seemed*
*so distant. Then I heard His voice. He said simply,*
*"It's about My love."*

Susannah had been going to university in the States. How had she gotten to Brussels? And how did Matthew arrive? How had Susannah gotten to the hospital? And Matthew? Why did they all come? Don't leave me for a moment! What is the hissing noise? Why can't I speak? I didn't want my children and Paul to leave me. I wanted them close. Susannah told me later that she held my hand and could see in my eyes that I didn't want her to go, even to the bathroom. What a dear and faithful daughter!

And O, Lord, have you left me? Where are you? I longed for the sense of His Presence, but God seemed so distant. And then, in my spirit, I heard His voice. He said simply, "It's about My love; it's about My love." It was like an anchor for my soul. I could feel myself stabilizing. Amid our suffering and pain His Word is like a solid rock, a stabilizer. I didn't understand things any more clearly, but I began to know somewhere in my soul that it was OK.

## ❧ Permission to Pull the Plug

*From Paul's Reflections*

In the early weeks after Rebecca's accident, the medical community—a fine, competent group—was not hopeful for her recovery. On day 12, surgery was scheduled to stabilize her neck. This involved inserting two long screws. The surgeon, a specialist with a good reputation, called me into his office.

After some introductory comments, I said that I wanted Rebecca to start physical therapy soon, since the immobility wasn't good for future movement. He interrupted me in the middle of my sentence to tell me, firmly, that Rebecca would never move again and never breathe on her own again. His goal in our meeting was to ask permission to pull the plug during the surgery if she got into a crisis.

I was angry! "I want her any way I can have her!" was my response. Then he became angry as well, but he knew my position.

Later that same day I asked another one of the ICU doctors, one who was most kind to us, if he agreed with the surgeon's prognosis. He hesitated, then said: "Well, Mr. Petrie, the best I can say is that she may have a one in 10,000 chance of improvement." It was very bleak at that moment.

A few days after the surgery we thought we saw the first faint movement in her left big toe. No one was sure that it was a voluntary movement, not even Rebecca. I again brought up the idea of physical therapy with the doctors. And again the response was not positive. So I went, by myself, up to the 6th floor physical therapy unit and brought down to ICU a large, metal physical therapy contraption on wheels that would extend over the bed with various ropes and pulleys.

> *"His goal in our meeting was to ask permission to pull the plug during surgery if Rebecca got into a crisis. I was angry! 'I want her any way I can have her!' was my response."*
>
> —*Paul*

Carefully, at least as carefully as I knew how to be, I put the pulleys under Rebecca's arms and legs and began slowly to move them. The doctors were, well…horrified! (Remember, she was in ICU on life support.) But they realized I was serious and called one of the physical therapists down, arranging for Rebecca to have daily therapy in ICU.

That little movement in her toe became slight movement in her left foot, then slight movement in her left hand. Today she can use her left hand to move the joy stick on her wheelchair, to eat, to hold a phone, to write, to gesture… She can even sit on the side of the bed for several minutes with the help of the physical therapist. In this position she can kick her legs, and rotate her upper body. These are significant accomplishments for someone who had had such a bleak early prognosis. "Through many dangers, toils, and snares we have already come. 'Tis grace that brought us safe thus far, and grace will lead us home" (John Newton).

## ❀ Two Steps Forward, One Step Back: Grounded in His Person

*From Paul, November 19, 2001*

Two steps forward; one step back! These have been three difficult days. Since the first surgery, Rebecca has been in significant pain and distress. Her nights have been long and hard. This afternoon the doctors tried to see if Rebecca could breathe at all on her own, but had to reintroduce the tracheotomy because of her inability to breathe or swallow. She cannot speak or eat, and will continue to be tube fed.

---

*"As we walk through a time like this, the pain and difficulty come wave after wave. Where do we turn our hearts? On what is our faith grounded? ... In times like this we must **know** Him." —Paul*

---

She also has extreme pain on the right side of her face and head. The doctors are saying there was some trauma during the surgery to the nerves going to her face. We just now understood that the new and "extreme pain" would be permanent. Trigeminal neuralgia!

As we walk through a time like this, the pain and difficulty come wave after wave. Where do we turn our hearts? On what is our faith grounded? Often there are days and events that are unexplainable to our rational mind. In times like these we must know Him. Our days must be grounded in our knowledge of the Lord, Himself. He is good and He is faithful.

## ❋ The Strength of His Word

*From Paul, December 09, 2001*

In seasons of darkness, God's Word is the strength and the source of our perspective. This has certainly been true in these last few days. Some verses in 1 Peter 4 and 5 from "The Message" have been so helpful:

> *Since Jesus went through everything you're going through and more, learn to think like him. Think of your suffering as a weaning from that old sinful habit of always expecting to get your own way. Then you'll be able to live out your days free to pursue what God wants instead of being tyrannized by what you want.*
>
> *Friends, when life gets really difficult, don't jump to the conclusion that God isn't on the job. Instead, be glad that you are in the thick of what Christ experienced.*
>
> *So keep a firm grip on the faith. The suffering won't last forever. It won't be long before this generous God who has great plans for us in Christ—eternal and glorious plans they are!—will have you put together and on your feet for good. He gets the last word; yes, he does.*

## DURING REHAB

At Pellenburg Rehabilitation Center after the time in ICU and Hospital, March 27, 2002 – April 11, 2003

### ❋ Mosquitoes and Feeding Tubes: God, both Strong and Loving

*From Rebecca*

*The attack came in the intense heat of the night, through the unscreened windows.*

I had a significant time with the Lord last night. It began with a mosquito attack. They came in the intense heat of the night, through the unscreened windows. Since I am not able to resist them in any way, I finally resolved myself to their fury, "Just bite me, then!" The same night, another event occurred. I am fed from a plastic container suspended over my head with a tube that goes directly into my stomach. In the middle of the night the container fell with a crash. It barely missed my head. The nurse ran in and was frantic in her concern and apologies. I was angry, but not with the nurse. I was angry with God!

I have often taught from Psalm 62: 11-12: "...two things have I heard: that you, O God, are strong, and that you, O Lord, are loving" (NIV). This Scripture is one on which I have based my life. I've taught that we serve a God who is both good and all-powerful. He is able to do all that His goodness requires. For years I have taught that if He is good but not able, or if He is able but not good, then we are in trouble.

As I lay there in the heat, I cried out to God, "I do not doubt that You are able, but I am not sure anymore that You are good." He replied immediately and clear-

> *As I lay there, I cried out to God, "I do not doubt that You are able, but I am not sure anymore that You are good." He replied immediately.*

ly, "Dear one, that attitude is wrong." His answer shocked me, and with His answer came repentance. I wept. In my tears God washed me with His love. Indeed, "You, O God, are strong, and You, O Lord, are loving."

## ❧ What is Your Secret?

*From Rebecca*

A few days ago the psychologist here at Pellenberg asked me, "What is your secret?" I was delighted to have the opportunity to say, it is Jesus, living in me. How do you bear the unbearable? Jesus! How do you endure the unendurable? Jesus! How do you find joy and contentment in the middle of terrible loss and pain? Jesus! He, Himself, is what we need. His grace is enough.

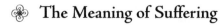 **The Meaning of Suffering**

> *"Despair is suffering without meaning."*
>
> —*Victor Frankl*
> *Nazi concentration camp survivor*

*From Paul, May 05, 2002*

The apostle Paul said that the outer person is perishing while the inner person is renewed day by day. There is a dichotomy here, but it is a freeing process. Jesus, not the circumstances of our lives, is the One who determines the atmosphere of our souls.

Victor Frankl, survivor of a Nazi concentration camp, expressed one of the crises faced by people who suffer: "Despair is suffering without meaning." The question of the meaning of suffering arises, almost viscerally. And it is a question that many, including we ourselves, have asked about the situation that Rebecca and I face. It seems relatively simple to find meaning in activity or productivity. But how do we find meaning in suffering? I believe it is only when our suffering leads us to God Himself. When God delivered Israel from Egypt, it wasn't principally to bring them into the land. It was to bring them to Himself. In Exodus 19:4, we read, "You have seen what I did to the Egyptians, and how I bore you on eagles' wings and brought you to Myself" (NKJV).

What is the meaning of suffering? Surely one of the great meanings is to bring us to Him, and free us from the tyranny of our lives' circumstances. He is our inheritance, our hope, our joy.

## Good Days and Bad Days

*From Paul, September 15, 2002*

One of the comments the medical staff give to a new patient arriving at Pellenberg, Rebecca's rehabilitation center, is: "There are good days and bad days." Isn't that the way life is? We're surprised, even shocked, when we have a "bad day," rather than remembering that God is still good, and tomorrow will be better.

Ecclesiastes 3:4 says there is a time for weeping. And Psalm 30:5 says that, "Weeping may endure for a night, but joy comes in the morning" (NKJV). I know that, in God's compassion, He draws near and shares our pain, knowing that a time will come when all tears will be wiped away. Until then, we have Him—and one another. Surely that is sufficient!

## DURING LONDON SURGERIES

The London surgeries took place during the time in rehab, July 11, 2002 – August 2, 2002

### ⚘ God's Prison Cell

*From Rebecca*

In the early days after my accident I felt the Lord refer to my being His "prisoner." That suffering, caused by my physical limitation, was for me His "prison cell."

My sister Judy has been here helping. This week she has been meditating on the apostle Paul's years in a Roman prison. She was struck that the believers around him prayed for his immediate release while they had no idea that the letters he was writing them would become the foundation of our faith 2000 years later. The apostle Paul was indeed "God's prisoner."

In the late 1600's Madam Guyon, a French noblewoman, was imprisoned because of her faith. She spent years in solitary confinement, in a prison that I can hardly imagine. This week I received from a friend, a poem that Madame Guyon wrote. This is just the first verse:

*A little bird I am,*
*Shut from the fields of the air,*
*And in my cage I sit and sing,*
*To Him who placed me there;*
*Well pleased a prisoner to be*
*Because, my God, it pleases Thee.*

In the early 1900's Amy Carmichael, missionary to India, became an invalid as a result of an accident. She was bedridden for the last 20 years of her life. Much of that time she was in great pain, and yet produced some of her most profound writing and poetry. She, too, saw these limitations as her prison. The last two verses of her poem, "Light in the Cell," based on Acts 12:7 read:

*Light of Love shined in the cell,*
*Turned to gold the iron bars,*
*Opened windows to the stars;*
*Peace stood there as sentinel.*

*Dearest Lord, how can it be*
*That Thou art so kind to me!*
*Love is shining in my cell,*
*Jesus, my Immanuel.*

The examples of these remarkable women have given me fresh courage. I've thought of the different "prison cells" that the Lord has given me in the past. Sometimes, I failed to recognize and receive them as from His hand. What a privilege and joy that He is my Jail Keeper and His name is Love. As the Psalmist says, He has stored up goodness for me today.

## ✤ Off to London

*From Paul, June 07, 2002*

Rebecca will need another surgery, possibly two, to stabilize her neck. She has been in Pellenberg, the physical therapy hospital, for some months now. It has just become evident that the early surgeries were not sufficient to stabilize her head. It appears they must remove the screws and wires that were put in during the second surgery, and do a complicated procedure of rebuilding the upper vertebrae with metal bars (these are my words, which may not be medically accurate). There are only two doctors in the world that do this delicate kind of surgery through the mouth. One is in London. The head of Neurosurgery here in Belgium will meet with him in Paris at an international consultation of Neurosurgeons in a few days. We are amazed at the goodness of God that this meeting "just happens" to be next weekend. Because of the unusual nature of Rebecca's case, she has been put on the agenda for this group. Please pray for them to have wisdom in these considerations.

Our Neurosurgeon will return to Brussels late next week, and I'll see him the early part of the following week. Meanwhile, Rebecca is not to be moved or to sit up. She will need to go to London for these surgeries. We don't have dates yet, but our doctor here said that the situation is urgent and will be expedited.

When I first requested your prayer—eight months ago—I said that this would be a long haul. I had no idea! It seems a miracle to me that Rebecca and I could be sitting here in peace facing such uncertainty. Your prayers are a vehicle for God's sustaining grace. We need them now more than ever.

One thing for sure: we will get through this. I just reminded Rebecca that the center of our lives, (our love for Jesus, for one another, and for all of you), is firm—and that IS life. The rest is just the "decoration."

## AT HOME

Home to stay, April 11, 2003

 **The Dead Sumac Tree**

*From Rebecca*

I'm sitting in my garden room looking out over "my beautiful trees." Right in the middle of our garden is a large old sumac tree. Two years ago it died and so, in the middle of the garden, we now have a beautifully shaped dead tree. Ivy is growing up and around the branches. I laugh and say it's my giant topiary. Again and again we've had people say, "Why don't

*The tree and the garden are a beautiful picture of my life: that which is gone and that which is springing forth, new life out of old, and beauty out of suffering where no one could have imagined.*

you take that tree out of there?" But somehow I like it.

At the base of the tree are growing three beautiful healthy baby sumacs. In a circle all around them are many lovely tall blue hydrangeas. This tree has become a symbol of my life. There is that which is dead and gone. But in and all around the tree is a celebration of life. The tree and the garden are a beautiful picture of my life: that which is gone and that which is springing forth, new life out of old, and beauty out of suffering where no one ever imagined.

## ❦ From Despair to Hope

*From Rebecca, May 07, 2004*

Recently I was talking with a friend who was in despair. She said, "My hopes have run out through the sieve of my discouragement and disappointment." Even though this well expressed my friend's feelings, I knew something was amiss in the sentiment. It set me on a search. What is hope?

I turned to Webster's Dictionary and found: "Hope is the highest degree of well-founded expectation of good." I remembered in Romans 5:3-5: "... we also rejoice in our sufferings, because we know that suffering produces perseverance; perseverance, character; and character, hope. And hope does not disappoint us, because God has poured out his love into our hearts by the Holy Spirit, whom he has given us" (NIV).

As I meditated on this, it seemed that suffering, rather than causing our hope to disappear, can produce hope. Could there be two different kinds of hope: a natural hope, and a spiritual hope? Through trials we often come to the end of our natural hopes, even hopes that are good. In the beginning this may result in disappointment, discouragement, and even despair. But as we hold on to the Lord, we persevere. I find that this perseverance works character in me. And, almost without realizing it, a new hope is born within my soul. It is Jesus Himself, His life, and His love "being poured out in my heart."

For many of us, we have come through or are still in circumstances in which our natural hope is being tested, and even drained away. But, oh, as we persevere, what a great treasure it is to have fresh hope that will never disappoint us, rooted in the Father's love. If you haven't read the first part of Romans 5 lately, read it again and see the riches God has for you there!

## ❀ Joy Out of Pain

*From Paul, July 03, 2003*

I have thought often of the idyllic world that our Father originally created, with such hope and promise. Then came the misfortune of the fall, and all the resulting pain and distortion. In the story of creation, Adam and Eve focused blame rather than love on each other. The first man born on earth became a brother killer. There was great loss on every hand, especially for our Father. And yet, He, at great personal sacrifice, has brought redemption and joy out of that tragedy.

---

*David said: "I would have perished if I had not believed in the goodness of God in the land of the living."*
Psalm 27:13 (NKJV)

---

Life took a huge and tragic turn for us, for our family, and our friends, on October 4, 2001. Rebecca's accident turned our world upside down. Yet, the Father has worked such redemption and joy—and "it has not yet been revealed what we shall be" (1 John 3:2, NKJV).

Whatever the circumstances, there is always reason for hope and confidence. Life is so different from what Rebecca and I had imagined it would be. Yet in our loss, we have found great treasure. Amid change we have discovered more deeply the wonders of the One who never changes.

We find meaning in our future, not by looking back, not by longing for things as they were. That makes the present good insipid. David said: "I would have lost heart, unless I had believed that I would see the goodness of the Lord in the land of the living" (Psalm 27:13, NKJV). We have found the goodness of God in the land of the living, and look forward every day to what He will show of Himself, and what He will do. �֎

CHAPTER THREE

# Courage and Determination

*"Have I not commanded you? Be strong and of good courage; do not be afraid, nor be dismayed, for the Lord, your God is with you wherever you go."*

Joshua 1:9 (NKJV)

*"When I said, 'My foot is slipping,' Your love, O Lord, supported me. When anxiety was great within me, Your consolation brought joy to my soul."*

Psalm 94:18-19 (NIV)

*"Wait on the Lord; be of good courage, and He shall strengthen your heart; wait, I say, on the Lord!"*

Psalm 27:14 (NKJV)

HOW DOES ONE BEGIN TO FACE BLINDING PAIN AND weakness? Where does one begin? In the world around us, new life begins with a seed. Courage is one of the seeds from which new life grows.

People have said to me through the years, "You are such a brave woman." I have never felt courageous. I'm really afraid. We taught our children early on "Courage is doing what you must, even when you are afraid." During these days, I found myself in such weakness that I had to cry out to Father who gives courage, as the starting point. Out of my fear, somehow I began to feel the seed, which is courage, enabling me to begin to go on.

This part of the journey begins in the examination room where, in my terror and fear, Christ met me with His strength. I can feel even today the miracle of that strength. "I can do this—I can follow you—I'll be OK."

## DURING ICU AND THE HOSPITAL

Immediately after the accident, October 4, 2001 – March 27, 2002

### ❦ Extreme Pain: Jesus Going Before

It has been a difficult day. Because of the extensive, unexplained swelling in my throat, I had to have an examination in which they lowered a small scope through my nose, down into my throat. With this scope they were able to look and see the inside, trying to discover the source of the swelling. I found the whole procedure extremely painful. To my horror, the doctors said yesterday that they had to repeat the examination. I did not think I could bear it. As I waited, I was filled with fear and dread. I glanced over my left shoulder and sitting there was Jesus! He was young and handsome and so real. But, I was shocked to see that He had His head back

*To my horror, the doctors said yesterday that they had to repeat the examination. I did not think I could bear it. As I waited, I was filled with fear and dread.*

and someone was lowering the scope down His dear nose. He looked over at me and said simply, "I will always go before you." Isaiah 53:4 tells us that "Surely He has borne our grief and carried our sorrows..." (NKJV). In this experience I felt the reality of Christ going before me and I received the gift of His courage.

## ✤ Courage Born Out of Struggle

In the early weeks, as the doctors struggled to keep me alive, my family was struggling. They wanted to touch and communicate with me. But because of the respirator, I was unable to speak. The horrible hissing from the machine punctuated my every gasp for air. Paul thought of an idea of an alphabet card with each of the letters written in lines. Then, Matthew made the card on the computer. Someone would hold the card in front of me and say, "Line one, two, three..." Then I would blink my eyes at the correct line, and they would begin with the letters, "Letter a, b, c..." When they reached the letter that I wanted, again I would blink my eyes. Yes, it was long and strenuous, but effective.

*They would begin with the letters, 'Letter a, b, c...' When they reached the letter I wanted, I would blink my eyes.*

One afternoon, Susannah was struggling to understand me because I kept repeating the same letters. My letters made no sense to her. Thankfully, Matthew came in and rescued me. She said, "Matt, what she's spelling doesn't make any sense. She keeps spelling over and over, 'CNN.'" Matt exclaimed, "Susannah, she wants to watch the news!"

## ✤ Never Left Alone

Through these early weeks the hardest part for me was the night. The nurses would finish their rounds and I would be left "alone." I felt terrified; I had no way to communicate. I couldn't move even a finger to push a button, and I couldn't cry out for help. These nights were often punctuated

> *He looked at me and said, "Mrs. Petrie, are you afraid?" I blinked my eyes. "Are you afraid to be alone?" I blinked again. He said, "I'll be here for you." And the dear man came by every ten minutes.*

by horrible dreams of being trapped in burning buildings with no way to call for help.

One evening a nurse stopped by my bed. He looked at me and said, "Mrs. Petrie, are you afraid?" I blinked my eyes. He said, "Are you afraid to be alone?" I blinked again. He said, "I'll be here for you." And the dear man came by every ten minutes or so every night from then on while I was unable to communicate. In our fear, Father is able to send an "angel" with all the courage that we need.

## ❦ Trachea Tubes and Smiles: Breath of Life

I will never forget when the day finally came when they tried to remove the trachea tube. It took some time to wean me from the machine and prepare me to breathe on my own. I had almost suffocated several times and I was terrified that I would not be able to breathe. I knew, however, that I dared not show the doctors my fear. I wanted this thing out!

My smile became a mask to cover my terror. I prayed, "Lord, give me the courage and enable me. Let Your breath of life be mine." They slowly removed the trachea, just for a brief moment, to see how I would do. I will never forget that first gasp of air on my own. Struggling, I was doing it. I was breathing again. Those first gasps of air were such a gift from my Father's hand. It was a miracle. It still sweeps over me, how delicious is the freshness of air!

Often when we feel that we're suffocating and not sure we'll be able to take the next breath, or step, Father is there and He will meet us.

## ❦ Every Conclusion is Also a Beginning

*From Paul, October 17, 2003*

The events of the last several days have encouraged us. Realism and faith, or hope, are not opposing ideas. I think both faith and hope are in their best environment when we are in reality about our circumstances. As a family, we have a growing confidence that Rebecca will have measurable, if not total recovery.

Sunday we felt the Lord say to us that this is a new beginning. It is an end to one season. But every conclusion is also a beginning. We will see the Lord's faithfulness to us now. We will be strengthened in our relationship with Him and with one another.

## DURING REHAB

At Pellenburg Rehabilitation Center after the time in ICU and Hospital, March 27, 2002 – April 11, 2003

## ❦ The Daily Climb

This morning, as the nurse set me up with my pen and journal for my quiet time, the Lord gave me a prayer: "Teach me to climb!" This prayer has been growing in me for months. Many sent cards and encouragements compared rehabilitation to mountain climbing. One such card had a mountain on the front. I had it placed on my bulletin board as a daily reminder. Then the other evening I came across this poem, "Teach Me to Climb" by Amy Carmichael. I had forgotten that in her later years she compared her life to climbing a mountain.

*Let the stern array*
*Of the forbidding be a constant call*
*To fling into the climb my will, my all.*
*Teach me to climb.*

At each phase of my recovery, it was as if I were climbing to a new level on the mountain. Each level required courage. How thankful I am that the Holy Spirit is the Author and the Generous Giver of Courage for each stage of our journey.

## ❀ Courage from Discouragement

During occupational therapy (this is the program designed to prepare a patient to re-enter life after the hospital) last week there was a woman opposite me, who, with great effort had managed to get herself off the bench and into her wheelchair. The next day when I came in she was playing cards, dealing, handling the cards, enjoying her therapist. I said: "May I ask a question? How long have you been here? I'm so impressed with your progress." She smiled and said, "6 months." It helped me a lot to see my first two weeks in a longer prospective and gave me the courage to go on.

*God sees the beginning and the end and He knows all the steps I must take in between. When I look from my perspective, I become discouraged. Courage is always hidden in the word "discouragement."*

I am encouraged to remember that Father's perspective is different from mine. He sees the beginning and the end and He knows all the steps I must take in between. When I look from my prospective, I become discouraged. Courage is always hidden in the word "discouragement." And when I don't allow Father to show me His prospective, my courage is stolen and I become discouraged. But Father is faithful and His courage is always available when we turn to Him.

## AT HOME

Home to stay, April 11, 2003

### ✤ The Challenges of a New Life

Several years ago, the Lord gave me two phrases that have helped set the course for my life: "Change my mind, and teach me what is good." I had not thought of either of these requests for the last eighteen months. The other day I remembered them anew realizing that only the Lord could teach me how to live this new life. He must change my mind and let me see goodness from His perspective.

---

*Two key phrases for my life:*
*Change my mind. Teach me what is good.*

---

Last week gave me an opportunity to put this truth into practice. It was a beautiful spring day. Robert and Tracey, an American nurse and his wife, had come to support me in my early days at home. On this spring day Robert came over and said, "Let's go for a walk at the lake." The thought of being outside in my chair frightened me, which made me know that I needed to do it. So Robert, Tracey, Paul, and I went for my first "walk" in my wheelchair. It was the first time that I'd been outside as a handicapped person among those who were not disabled. I knew that if anyone felt awkward seeing me, it was my responsibility to smile and try to put him or her at ease. But it was not easy.

The cobblestones and path were bumpier than any of us had realized. By the time we got back to the car, I was tired and nauseated. In fact, I made it back just in time! Thank God for plastic basins! When it was all over, we laughed together and said that I needed more practice. We all agreed that the walk was a good beginning, and knew future walks would become easier and even delightful.

God changes our minds so we know that He is God! This is the beginning of finding the courage we need.

Throughout this experience, God was changing my mind and letting me see my new life from His perspective. Sometimes beginnings are difficult. I must approach the first "steps" with courage—and with expectation for all the goodness God has in store. These are challenging days but also they are days of growth and fruitfulness.

## ❈ Let Us Fix Our Eyes on Jesus

*From Paul, March 01, 2004*

I have a personal health report to give. Rebecca's thoughts will follow, as they are related to this recent development. I returned from an extended trip to North America on February 12th. Rebecca and I had our first "date" since her accident, just the two of us, on Valentine's Day, the 14th.

We celebrated the 40th anniversary of our engagement. Then on Monday, February 16th, on the way into Brussels, I had a mini-stroke, followed by 2 more after I returned home. At my doctors' suggestion, I was taken to the hospital and admitted. The following day I had another episode, which left me with some limited movement in my left hand and droopiness on the left side of my mouth. Five days of intensive exams followed. The doctors were not able to identify the source, but think that some blood had clotted in one of the upper chambers of my heart and had broken loose, going to my brain. Each episode resulted in short-term loss of speech ability. That is behind me now. I've been home from the hospital for about

> *"Rebecca and I had our first "date" since her accident, just the two of us, on Valentine's Day. Then on Monday, February 16th, on the way into Brussels, I had a mini-stroke, followed by 2 more after I returned home."*
>
> —Paul

a week, and have canceled my next several international trips, both to recover, and to listen to the Lord.

While in the hospital I read Hebrews 12:1-3 again: "...let us run with perseverance the race marked out for us. Let us fix our eyes on Jesus, the author and perfecter of our faith...Consider him..." (NIV). I greatly appreciated this commanded point of focus: Jesus. Faith is what we live by, but Jesus is the author and perfecter of our faith. Our job is to keep eyes, hearts and minds fixed firmly on Him, and to view all our circumstances through Him. I'm so grateful the Father has made Jesus the center of all things.

*From Rebecca*

As you can imagine, the events which Paul has just recounted were difficult for me. It is surely harder when the Lord allows our loved ones to be afflicted, than when He does the same for us.

The evening that Paul spent in the E.R., Tracy and Judy stayed with me. (Robert and Stephen were with Paul.) I had moments of weeping, and moments of rest and faith—wavering between the two.

> *Jesus made the disciples go into the storm and Jesus is in our storm. Oh how could I forget! "Take courage! It is I, don't be afraid."*

The next morning as I awakened, it was such a sick feeling realizing that my beloved was in the hospital. I went to the Lord, and happened to be reading in Matthew 14. It is always a wonder to me that He is so faithful to meet us wherever we are. I came to verse 22 where it says Jesus made the disciples get into the boat and go ahead of Him into the rough seas to the other side. The Bible says the waves and wind were against them. Then He came walking to them across the water. When they saw Him, they didn't recognize Him and were terrified. "It's a ghost," they cried. In the middle of the storm, in the middle of their fear, they couldn't see clearly. Verse 27 says: "But Jesus immediately said to them: 'Take courage! It is I, don't be afraid'" (NIV).

When I read this, I was touched that He made them go into the storm; and He was in the storm. I realized once again that Jesus is in our storm. Oh, how could I forget! "Take courage! It is I, don't be afraid." With those words, peace came to me, such quietness of soul.

I thought of all of you, and what your storms might be, and prayed for you. "Lord, help us to see You in the storm, however great or small. When You are there, then we are at peace."

## ✦ What Happens Today Prepares Us for Tomorrow

*From Rebecca, May 23, 2006*

This past week I was talking with one of my nurses. I was glad Susannah was with me, because she was able to help me with my French when the ideas became too complex. My nurse began to tell about a new patient who had suffered a terrible accident and was now a paraplegic. As she spoke, her eyes filled with tears, and she said: "It makes me afraid of what might happen tomorrow. I know that some people go to fortune-tellers—and I understand why. But I wouldn't want to do that."

---

*My best preparation for tomorrow is in walking in Jesus' purpose for me today.*

---

I responded to her by sharing the importance of walking closely with the Lord day by day. "When we belong to Him," I said, "whatever happens today prepares us for tomorrow." I have had so many people ask me how I was able to adjust as I have to my own situation. One is not able, suddenly, to accept difficult things. Yet, day by day the Lord prepares us for whatever good or difficult conditions arise. My best preparation for tomorrow is in walking in Jesus' purpose for me today.

David said, in Psalm 31:14-15: "But as for me, I trust in You, O Lord;

I say, 'You are my God. My times are in Your hand...'" (NKJV). What a comfort it is, and joy, that we can rest confident because the One who holds our times in His hands loves us dearly. God loves us even more than we love our own children.

> *We are safe in His hands, even in the face of unpredictable weather patterns, terrorists, and unstable political systems.*

It's been a special season for us to have Susannah with us. As I looked at her this morning, mulling over some of these ideas, the sunlight came across her golden hair, highlighting her square cheekbone. I was amazed at her beauty. I realized, if I had the ability to order her day today, knowing what tomorrow would hold, so that she would be prepared for whatever lies ahead, how carefully I would do it. How I would orchestrate, plan, and protect her, keeping her for the highest and best.

If that is how I feel, as Jesus said: "If you then, being evil, know how to give good gifts to your children, how much more will your Father who is in heaven give..." (Matthew 7:11 NIV). We are safe in His hands, even in the face of unpredictable weather patterns, terrorists, and unstable political systems. We are safe. By walking with Him today, we'll be ready for tomorrow.

### ❀ Developing New Endurance

*From Rebecca, July 28, 2006*

I've been through a period of not sleeping well for the first time since my accident. I was becoming more and more tired. The other morning Melissa Christensen, a young friend (16 years old) was helping with my morning care. I said to her: "Oh, Melissa, I'm just so tired." She said: "Rebecca, that's great! The Lord must be developing new endurance in you. That's what it says in James. Our trials develop endurance."

I said, "Oh, Melissa, say it again!" She said it, and I said once more, "I think I need to hear it again. Please say it once more."

That night I was again too warm in my bed. (You see, when I'm in my bed and I get too hot or cold, there is almost nothing I can do about it myself. Since I have only partial use of one hand and arm, I'm just able, in a limited fashion, to push my covers down a little. I do have a button that I can push and call either Annie or Susannah, depending who's on call that night. But I hate to do that. As my caregivers, who also have many other responsibilities, they are often weary. I know what it means to them to be awakened, so I try not to call them if I can possibly help it.) That morning, I could tell by the light coming through the drapes and the birdsongs that it was close to the time when they would come to get me up. Sometimes someone comes a little early, so I began to pray for this. Often I spend that time in fruitful prayer, but that morning I could only pray for someone to come! In the heart of my prayer the Lord said to me: "You're looking for deliverance, not endurance"—after all the lessons of the day before!

> *I said, "Oh Melissa, say it again!" She said it, and I said it once more, "I think I need to hear it again. Please say it once more."*

You can imagine that as they were preparing me to go down into the garden for my time with the Lord, I asked to have my Bible open at James 1, that I might meditate on those words to which Melissa had referred.

This portion of Scripture is underlined and marked with many notations, because it is one that has meant so much to me through the years. I've studied it in the JB Phillip's translation. At one point I memorized it. But that morning, as I meditated on it, I saw a picture in my mind. I saw myself with a circle drawn around me. It was a circle that represented the extent of my faith. Within that circle I was comfortable and my faith was strong. Then I saw the Lord take me outside that circle into another area. I was shaky and uncomfortable. I realized that my faith level wasn't up for this new experience. I had to endure being uncomfortable until He worked in me a new level of faith. In the progression, my circle was getting bigger and bigger.

*Sometimes we are looking for deliverance when God wants us to learn endurance.*

Oh Lord, give us willing hearts to recognize the trials that You send as opportunities to grow in faith and endurance, as we become all that You would have us become. The Phillip's translation of James 1:2-5 says: "When all kinds of trials and temptations crowd into your lives, don't resent them as intruders, but welcome them as friends! Realize that they come to test your faith and to produce in you that quality of endurance. But let the process go on until that endurance is fully developed, and you will find that you have become men of mature character, men of integrity with no weak spots." �֎

CHAPTER FOUR

# Letting Go: Loss With Thankfulness

*"What is more, I consider everything a loss
compared to the surpassing greatness of
knowing Christ Jesus my Lord, for whose
sake I have lost all things. I consider them
rubbish, that I may gain Christ and be
found in him, not having a righteousness of
my own that comes from the law, but that
which is through faith in Christ—the
righteousness that comes from God and
is by faith."*

Philippians 3:8-9 (NIV)

*"Be anxious for nothing, but in everything by prayer and supplication, with thanksgiving, let your request be made known to God; and the peace of God, which surpasses all understanding, will guard your hearts and your minds in Christ Jesus."*

Philippians 4:6-7 (NKJV)

DURING THE EARLY DAYS AFTER MY FALL, LIFE WAS A dark blur. I was aware of all that was going on around me, but I was unable to communicate with my loved ones. Only being able to blink my eyes, I was trapped in the body that had served me so well for fifty-six years. How had this happened to me? What was it going to mean? How much better it would be to go on and be with the Lord, and yet—could I adjust to live like this, the horror of it, and where was the Lord?

There was not a sense of His presence, only vague realities. Out of the swirl I began to hear His voice, "It's about My love. It's about My love." I knew Him well. Deep in my soul was the reality that the Lord was good, and He loved me, whatever I was feeling or not feeling. But the pain was so intense; there was so much confusion, and there was such terrible loss. Where do I anchor my soul?

"Thank you, Lord." Somewhere from deep within my heart came the words, and with them, peace. "Thank you, Lord. Thank you, Lord. Whatever, You are good, Your love unchanging, and I am Yours to do whatever You would. Thank you, Lord."

In the face of my monumental loss, there came release through thankfulness. In 1 Thessalonians 5:18, Paul said, "give thanks in all circumstances..." (NIV). Somehow in my desperation and emptiness, I cried out, "Thank You, Lord." In thankfulness, I was able to begin to let go. I could accept my loss, and reach into the heavens and bring down the reality that even in this, Father was there. He was good and He was still in control of my life.

## DURING ICU AND THE HOSPITAL
Immediately after the accident, October 4, 2001 – March 27, 2002

### ❦ "There's No Place to Go Without You"

During the time I could not communicate, Paul reached out to share with all our friends. He shared his own suffering and both of our needs as best he could.

As soon as I was able to communicate, one of the first things I mouthed to him was, "Darling, I can't bear for you to be stuck with all of this. I release you if you need to go." I'll never forget his face. He looked at me with tears in his eyes and said, "Rebecca, there's no place to go without you. I'm here. And I will be here."

As I look back on that special moment and see it in perspective, I realize how important it was to let go. Often it is in letting go that we're able to receive back what God has for us. How thankful I am for his faithfulness to stand with me through that time. When I see today the fullness of the life we have together, I realize Father and Paul's wonderful faithfulness, standing with me to fulfill God's purpose.

> *I'll never forget his face. He looked at me with tears in his eyes and said, "Rebecca, there's no place to go without you. I'm here. And I will be here."*

### ❦ Being Thankful in All Things

*From Paul, October 27, 2001*

Susannah told me yesterday that Rebecca prayed out loud for the first time. Through the years, the Lord had taught Rebecca the importance of continuously giving thanks. 1 Thessalonians 5:18 tells us the will of God

*"Thanksgiving for all things is not the same as resignation. It brings God into the center of everything. Father is here. Thanksgiving focuses us on Him as our principal reality."*—Paul

for us is to give thanks in all things. Ephesians 5:20 says: "...always giving thanks to God the Father FOR everything in the name of our Lord Jesus Christ" (NIV, emphasis added). Susannah said that her mother thanked the Lord for her fall, for her paralysis, for her pain... Rebecca is remarkable!

Thanksgiving for all things isn't the same as resignation. It brings God into the center of everything. Father is here. Thanksgiving focuses us on Him as our principal reality. Rebecca is in the Lord's hands. She has great expectation of what He will, in His goodness, do through what lies ahead.

## The Grace of Relinquishment

*From Paul, November 20, 2001*

The ENT (Ear, Nose, and Throat) specialist did an hour's investigatory procedure with scopes. He was trying to find out the source of the problem in Rebecca's throat. Her throat is swollen completely shut. The doctors were unable to even insert a feeding tube through her nose down her throat. What they are now concluding, after another review of the scan, is the screws recently inserted in the neck protrude between 2 and 3 millimeters beyond the vertebrae into the soft tissue. This clearly is the cause of the swelling and of the face pain.

She is being fed intravenously now, and we are again using the alphabet card for her to spell her requests. All we can do is wait for the swelling to lessen.

Through the day I have seen so many emotions in her eyes: pain, weariness, some dread of the procedure, disappointment—then I have watched her process; I have watched the grace of God at work in her as she processed and again arrived at a place of peace. Derek Prince called it "the grace of relinquishment." When I left, she smiled her inimitable smile. She is "nestling, not wrestling."

## ❀ Enduring the Unendurable

*From Paul, December 04, 2001*

Rebecca's spirits are better—just a little weepy over not being able to provide us all with Christmas. As many of you know, she is a "Christmas person." Our house at this time of year is a wonderland. She said, in tears, "It's another thing I can lay at Jesus' feet." But we'll celebrate His birth nonetheless, and with great joy. I decided last evening, with Matt's encouragement, to put up some decorations in the house for the sake of the boys.

I want to close this update with a passage from Colossians 1 in "The Message" that has been meaningful for us both these last days:

*"We pray that you will have the strength to stick it out over the long haul—not the grim strength of gritting your teeth, but the glory-strength God gives. It is strength that endures the unendurable and spills over into joy, thanking the Father who makes us strong enough to take part in everything bright and beautiful that he has for us"*
Colossians 1 (The Message).

## DURING REHAB

At Pellenburg Rehabilitation Center after the time in ICU and Hospital,
March 27, 2002 – April 11, 2003

### ✤ Finding a New Life

One of the recent wonderful developments that I've experienced is the ability again to read my Bible for myself. It is wonderful. My nurses prop it up with pillows and help me get my reading glasses on. One nurse always drops a tissue into my hand and quietly closes the door. Last Sunday morning I was reading in Matthew 10, when I got to verse 39:

> *"He who finds his life will lose it, but he who loses his life for My sake will find it." It was as if I'd never read it before.*
>
> Matthew 10:39 (NKJV)

"He who finds his life will lose it, but he who loses his life for My sake will find it" (NKJV), it was as if I'd never read it before.

I have lost a life. But in the coming months, I will be finding a new life in His good plan and purpose.

Just a few days earlier, Paul and I had discussed the possibility of a new bedroom on our house. This was the first time I had been able to imagine a place for me in the future.

The next day, when the doctors made their rounds, they talked, for the first time, about my working toward going home every weekend—with the goal of going home permanently by the spring. It was a shock to me. I had the emotional response of feeling that they wanted to get rid of me. Looking back, I can see that I thought I would always be institutionalized. I felt I could only be comfortable in the hospital and I could hardly imagine myself at home. Then I remembered, "finding a new life," and joy filled my heart. Isn't His Word and the timing of it remarkable? God's kindness and goodness continually catch up with me and overwhelm me.

## ✤ Covered with the Umbrella of Thanksgiving

"Give thanks in all circumstances, for this is God's will for you in Christ Jesus" (1 Thessalonians 5:17, NIV). Years ago, Paul told me the Greek in this passage means to "cover all things with the umbrella of thanksgiving.'" I'm always amazed at how I can forget lessons that over the years, the Lord has made a part of the foundation of my walk with Him.

This week I made a discovery of just such an area. I've been having a noticeable loss of dexterity in my left hand (my good hand). I seem to have less control, although my mobility is still good. When I talk to the doctors about it, they can't see much of a change. And besides, they don't know what to do about it, since they don't know why I can use my left hand at all.

The Lord showed me that I was worrying about it. Over 30 years ago the Lord taught us to exchange worry for thanksgiving. John Wesley said: "I would rather curse and swear than worry." It has been such a joy to live a life full of thanksgiving, knowing that the God of love was in control, and was sending good things. But in these last weeks, worry has crept in. I asked the Lord to forgive me, and decided that every time I noticed any change in my left hand, I would thank Him and praise Him for His goodness. I am covered, and I am His. I'm so thankful that we are able to be a people whose hearts are full of thanksgiving and gratitude.

## ✤ When the Seasons Change

*From Paul, November 20, 2002*

I've been meditating on the different seasons in life: times when we act (are led to take initiatives) and times when we are acted upon. In Jesus' early ministry He took initiative, led His disciples, confronted the Pharisees, did what He saw His Father doing. Then the season shifted and He was moved along by others, by events. He saw this too as part of the Father's plan; the Father had "delivered" Him into this new circumstance.

Jesus told Peter that he would also later face this same process. A time would come when he'd be led where he did not want to go. The apostle Paul had that experience: seasons of great initiatives and latitude, then seasons of limitation with things imposed on him that he would not have chosen.

It is important to know which season we're in. To know whether the Father is giving to us to be active, or to be acted upon.

Different seasons demand different responses, different anticipations, and a different exercise of faith.

Rebecca and I have obviously experienced the change from taking many initiatives to being carried along by unforeseen events. Jesus navigated these waters motivated by His love for the Father, and His love for us. He was serving the Father, not His own life and ministry. Paul said that he went through difficult seasons with a view to the benefit they would be to others, not to the effect on him personally. The last couple of verses of a poem I read recently helped me in this perspective:

> *For strength to bear is found in duty done;*
> *And it is best indeed to learn to make*
> *The joy of others cure one's own heartache.*
> —*L.B. Cowman, Streams in the Desert*

Each season has its particular service. Please pray that I'll be able to be a consistent source of strength and joy to Rebecca and our children. They are the first ones who need my life and love.

## AT HOME

Home to stay, April 11, 2003

### ❀ Good Plans for a Future

Coming home from Pellenberg last weekend, we came to the little lake where Paul and I walked for many years. My mind went back to our walks, to eating together in some of the restaurants that circle the lake, and I felt sad. I carried that sense of sadness through the evening. The next morning in my devotional time the Lord brought it back to my mind, and gently reminded me to let go of the past and embrace in faith the things that He had planned.

I thought of the Scripture from Luke 9:62: "No one who puts his hand to the plow and looks back is fit for service in the Kingdom of God" (NIV).

Surely there is an important place in our lives for remembering, with thanksgiving, but when that remembering turns to a longing for what is past, it can become sin. I was given the precious gift of repentance. I wept, realizing that the Lord desired for me to look ahead and not back. What has been, has been His gift to me, but no more so than what will be! That too is

> *"For I know the plans I have for you,"* declares the Lord, *"plans to prosper you and not to harm you, plans to give you a hope and a future."*
> Jeremiah 29:11 (NIV)

His gift to me. I'm reminded of the scripture in Jeremiah 29:11: "For I know the plans I have for you,' declares the Lord, 'plans to prosper you and not to harm you, plans to give you hope and a future'" (NIV).

## Releasing our Treasures

Releasing and letting go has been an important part of every area of my life. In my weakened condition, you would think the Lord would ease up on me. Still I must release my life and all that I have to Him. In no place have I felt it more keenly than in relationship to our children. I must release them into the hand of God for they are His, not ours!

On the back page of my Bible, I have each of the children named with the Scriptures the Lord has given me in their growing up years. Each one represents a letting go. Maybe it is an acknowledgment of to Whom they belong.

I remember when our Matthew was a teenager. I needed to release him and I was struggling! The Lord said to me, "I'm praying for him." What a relief!

Then when we left Susannah at university for the first time, on the way home we cried, and reminisced, and cried, and reminisced some more.

After we got home, I was fine. People said to me that they were surprised that I was not having more of an adjustment to my only daughter being away from home. I realized that leaving her and releasing her to university was not so difficult because I'd been releasing her throughout her whole life.

Several weeks ago, our Phillip was home for a short time. He sat on my bed and we laughed and prayed together. It was one of the sweetest times we'd ever had. Then he had to leave to return to North America to begin his university. I chose to leave him in the hands of the One who loves him more than his dad and I do.

*"He will have no fear of bad news; his heart is steadfast, trusting in the Lord. His heart is secure, he will have no fear; in the end, he will look in triumph on his foes. He has scattered abroad his gifts to the poor, his righteousness endures forever..."*

Psalm 112 :7-8 (NIV)

As I am writing this chapter, all of this is fresh in my mind because our "baby," Stephen, is in the Democratic Republic of Congo. He left with friends who were going on a mission trip. They speak no French and needed someone to translate. It was decided that Stephen would go. Before Stephen left, Paul was in the States and I was struggling: "We're going to send our baby, 17 years old, into a war zone. We've got to be crazy." I struggled with it all night. Have you noticed that situations are always much worse in the middle of the night? In the morning I wakened and said to the Lord, "OK, if You don't change my mind by the time Paul gets home tomorrow, I'm going to say that this child cannot go to Africa. I have no peace about it."

Then I went into my quiet time. These days I always begin in the Psalms. I was in Psalm 107, and the Lord said: "No, not there." I kept turning the pages until I got to Psalm 112. He said, "There!" In verses 7-8 it says, "He will have no fear of bad news; his heart is steadfast, trusting in the Lord. His heart is secure, he will have no fear; in the end, he will look in triumph on his foes. He has scattered abroad his gifts to the poor, his righteousness endures forever..." (NIV).

I realized the thing I feared was bad news. And when I read about scattering our gifts to the poor, Stephen is our most precious gift, and Congo is the poorest of the poor. I knew the Lord was in it, and that I could trust Him to bring about His purpose.

##  A Whole New Life

*From Rebecca, October 19, 2004*

On the morning of October 4th I said to my nurse: "Today is my anniversary." In French the word "anniversary" can mean birthday, so the nurse responded by saying "Happy Birthday."

I said, "Oh, no! It's not my birthday. It is the anniversary of my accident."

"I'm so sorry," she said.

"Don't be sorry," I responded. "The first two years were full of great difficulty. But we've passed through that. And who, at my age, gets to have a whole new life?" I went on then to share with this particular nurse, for the first time, how good the grace and purpose of God is. That evening we had a small dinner party here at home with several friends. I couldn't help but marvel at where I have come, compared with where I had been.

##  A Little Bird Began to Sing

*From Rebecca, February 23, 2006*

The last days before Paul's return (from a trip to the U.S.) were difficult and somewhat stressful. This left me drained, vulnerable, and weary. I found myself facing anew the reality of my present "prison"—longing to walk up our street, or around the lake, and feel spring beginning to come. I wanted to go and visit my children, and felt so desperately the ocean between us.

Then one morning I wakened and, before the dawn broke, a little bird began to sing. Its warbling notes spoke to me of spring, and thankfulness began to fill my soul. Oh, such thankfulness for Paul's love and care. And I'm grateful for Annie's gentle administration. And I am blessed by Judy's constant love and service. I am thankful for all those who care for my needs; for all of you who pray and carry me, even through these dark moments. I am thankful for our children; and thankful most of all for the reality in my soul of the Lord Himself. As this thankfulness continued to well up within me, joy replaced the darkness of the days before. His call and purpose for my life today overwhelmed the longing for that which I don't have.

I remembered what He had spoken to us years ago through C.S. Lewis: to guard our hearts, setting them firmly on what He has given, not sending them after what is not ours for today. When I long for that which I don't have, it destroys my joy!

May the Lord make us a people who are filled with gratefulness and thankfulness for that which we have, for what He has given.

*"Be anxious for nothing, but in everything, by prayer and supplication, with thanksgiving, let your requests be made known to God."*

Philippians 4:6 (NKJV)

CHAPTER FIVE

# *Waiting on God*

"*Truly my soul silently waits for God;*
*from Him comes my salvation.*
*My soul, wait silently for God alone,*
*For my expectation is from Him.*
*God has spoken once, twice*
*I have I heard this:*
*That power belongs to God.*
*Also to You, O Lord,*
*belongs mercy (love)...*"

Psalm 62:1, 5, 11 & 12 (NKJV)

"STAY WITH ME. STAY WITH ME." IT WAS A VOICE FAR away and then through a tunnel of light there was a face. I'd never seen him before. He kept encouraging me, "Stay with me. Stay with me."

The accident had just occurred. I was a crumpled body at the bottom of the stairs—the pain was severe. What had happened? What were they doing? Reality faded in and out. Breathing was almost impossible. Paul was there with me, but what could have happened? "Lord, where are You?"

> *I was a crumpled body at the bottom of the stairs—the pain was severe. It was October 4th and I had just begun what was to become the longest "wait on God" of my life.*

It was October 4th, and I had just begun what was to be the longest "wait on God" of my life. It was a new "adventure." One in which I would discover new dimensions of the Lord Himself, of His goodness and love, the kindness of many people, and a new life as a quadriplegic. But these discoveries would only come through a long period of waiting before Him.

As I later reflected on this time, I realized that I never had what so many describe as an "out-of-body experience." My "tunnel of light" directed me back to the face of a stranger—the head doctor from the emergency room of the local hospital. I've wondered if the Lord, with a twinkle in His eye, said to one of His angels, "Her work for Me there is not finished and I'm afraid if she gets close, she'll try to slip right in."

The long wait for my new life ahead had just begun.

## DURING ICU AND THE HOSPITAL

Immediately after the accident, October 4, 2001 – March 27, 2002

 ### Enlarged in the Waiting

*From Paul, November 24, 2001*

Romans 8 tells us that nothing can separate us from the love of God—

nothing. My how grateful we are for that reality! In the same chapter (The Message) the apostle Paul says, "We are enlarged in the waiting." Our family is being enlarged in this waiting, hopefully to contain more of Him.

This is an active waiting with anticipation toward Him, with confidence the Lord is working. We want to avoid disappointment. It sours the present. I told Rebecca the other day that life with her is wonderful regardless of the circumstances. And that is true!

 ## Lord, Enable Me!

The therapist wheeled me into my room after physical therapy and pushed the bell for the nurses to come and put me in bed. As I sat there, I was already past my endurance for being in the chair. I felt shaky and nauseated. I prayed, "Lord, please send those nurses quickly." I continued waiting, 5 minutes, then 10. I felt like I had gone way beyond my ability. Then I began to pray, "Lord give me grace to sit here. You are teaching me; give me Your grace to extend my time." And I remembered, "Lord I'm waiting on You. As I wait on You, You will strengthen me. Your grace will come." Just a small turn of the prism where the light shines through in a different way and shows a different perspective! My perspective changed from "Lord, save me!" to "Lord, enable me!" And that's what He did.

---

*"And God is able to make ALL grace abound to you, so that in ALL things at ALL times, having ALL that you need, you will abound in EVERY good work."*

2 Corinthians 9:8 (NIV, emphasis added)

---

=====

*People in hospitals are called "patients." If there is anything they need to be...it is patient!*

=====

## DURING REHAB

At Pellenburg Rehabilitation Center after the time in ICU and Hospital,
March 27, 2002 – April 11, 2003

 **Patients and Patience**

This week I have thought a lot about people in hospitals who are called "patients." If there is anything they need to be it is patient. In the last eleven-and-a half months I've spent most of my time waiting: for nurses, for doctors, for breakfast, for my medicines, for exams, and for treatments.

But I had a new thought last weekend. Twenty-six years ago, when I was in the last month of pregnancy (that time when it feels like you've been pregnant all your life), the Lord spoke and said: "I would speak to you of waiting." He's been speaking to me about waiting since then. Isn't it funny that I have never thought of it in relation to my waiting in the hospitals? This thought began when I found a card that Susannah sent me in June. She wrote the verses from Psalm 62:5-6:

*"My soul, wait silently for God alone, for my expectation is from Him. He only is my rock and my salvation; He is my defense...*
*Trust in Him at all times,*
*you people; pour out your heart before Him; God is a refuge for us."*
Psalm 62: 5-8 (NKJV)

As I read this familiar Scripture, I realized that while I am waiting, I'm not waiting for the nurse, or the medicine, or the treatment. I am waiting for my Father. He has all power, all mercy, and all love.

Andrew Murray, in his book, *Waiting on God*, says that we begin waiting for our spouse to be saved, for a job promotion, for a child to find the Lord (for a nurse or for a doctor). But after a while, we realize that what God is after is for us to learn to wait on Him. Waiting is such an important part of life. It is also an important part of our walk with God. How thankful I am for these new opportunities, each day, to wait on Him.

 **Feeding on Him**

*From Paul, June 06, 2002*

Here's what fed me this morning:

*"There is far more to this life than trusting in Christ. There is also suffering for him. And the suffering is as much a gift as the trusting. Anyone who wants to live all-out for Christ is in for a lot of trouble; there's no getting around it. Think of your sufferings as a weaning from that old sinful habit of always expecting to get your own way. Then you'll be able to live out your days free to pursue what God wants instead of being tyrannized by what you want."*

Verses from Philippians, 2 Timothy, and 1 Peter
(The Message)

Our souls need to be fed every day. Yesterday's bread might be stale, but it still has some food value. But remembering yesterday's meal has no nourishment at all. I, for one, have to "feed on Him" everyday to have strength for what each day holds.

 ## The Spirituality of Waiting

*From Paul, November 18, 2002*

This is from The Message, Proverbs 3, "...don't try to figure out everything on your own. Listen for God's voice in everything you do, everywhere you go; He's the One who will keep you on track." One of the French versions says: "He is the One who will act."

A friend of mine recently sent me two tapes by Henri Nouwen on "The Spirituality of Waiting." He identifies my struggle with this waiting—since the decisions before us seem so pressing. But the gift of this moment is uncertainty—not clarity. Nouwen says that waiting means being "present to the moment." For me that means being "present" to the unknown, to the inability to act, or decide, or prepare the future for Rebecca—not a comfortable place. But He is the One who must reveal, and who must act. For now, waiting is what is given me.

*"My soul waits for the Lord...*
*For with the Lord is unfailing love*
*and with him is full redemption."*
Psalm 130: 6-7 (NIV)

 ## Waiting in Hope

*From Paul, Notes from September 11, 2002 (sent out on October 01)*

Today is 9/11. I just arrived home and turned on the BBC. It is

*Much has changed for us. The wife and mother who is so central to our lives, hasn't been in our home for a year. Her function has changed. My, and our, love for Rebecca has only deepened. Though she is not here in our home, she is still central to our lives, and home is where she is.*

Remembrance Day! Like most of us, I remember where I was when terrorists struck the Twin Towers. Rebecca and I were in Kinshasa. The cell phone rang. It was Mary, my secretary, asking if we had heard what was happening. We had not. She began describing, live, what she was watching on CNN. Horror and surrealism gripped me! As the day progressed we traveled across town to the home of friends who had access to CNN. Glued to the events, we watched with disbelief and our senses rejected the reality we were seeing. There was the knowledge the world, as we had known it, was changing.

In many ways, October 4th was, for us, a reliving of 9/11. It was the day our lives were changed—the day of Rebecca's accident. As I called each of our children from the hospital that day, there were similar emotions of incredulity and surrealism. There was a similar visceral rejection of the reality into which we had just been plunged. At the same sense, I knew that life would permanently change because of this event.

America has gone on and faced the processes of recovery with hope and determination. Our family, likewise, has gone on with the determination to hold to the One who is the source of hope.

Much has changed for us. The wife and mother who is so central to our lives, hasn't been in our home for a year. Her function has changed. Yet, much hasn't changed! First, the love and goodness of God, rooted in His good and loving character, haven't changed. My, and our, love for Rebecca has only deepened. Though she is not here in our home, she is still central to our lives, and home is where she is.

Yesterday in the hospital, I said to her: "Whatever it holds, the future will be good, and we'll face it with anticipation." It will be a different "good" than we had imagined, but good nonetheless. There is a song that says: "God is good all the time." That can be construed as superficial and unrealistic—or it can be the testimony of eternal reality. In our minds and lives, the latter is true. He is indeed good—all the time. One year after Rebecca's accident, we want to thank God for His faithfulness and goodness. Our focus is on the future. We find joy in the One who is our life. The same power that raised Jesus from the dead, that brought His broken, lifeless body surging back from the grave, is the life that also lives in Rebecca. We pray that same power will surge into her physical body, continuing the restoration. We "wait in hope."

I want to close with a passage from Colossians 1 that has become a reality in us:

> *"We pray that you'll have the strength to stick it out over the long haul—not the grim strength of gritting your teeth but the glory-strength God gives. It is strength that endures the unendurable and spills over into joy...."*
> Colossians 1 (The Message)

## AT HOME

Home to stay, April 11, 2003

 **The Heart of My Life**

Psalm 25:4-5 says, "Show me your ways, O Lord, teach me Your paths. Lead me in Your truth and teach me, for You are the God of my salvation; on You I wait all day" (NKJV).

The note in my New King James Bible says, "Cultivating the knowledge of God requires the discipline of waiting on Him. As it's used here, 'wait' means 'to bind together through a process of intertwining,' clearly suggesting the virtual envelopment of the soul with God."

I didn't know how to live this new life. So I began to seek the Lord that He would teach me how to do it. I knew Father knew how one lived as a quadriplegic and He could show me how to do that as I waited on Him day by day.

Surely the heart of my life is the morning hour in my garden with Father, quietly waiting on Him. Allowing Him to bring me into His Presence and teach me to hear His voice. In that time, He faithfully envelops my soul and wraps me in Himself. What higher calling—it's difficult even to write it, allowing you to peek into my private world. I'm humbled and in awe as I touch the beauty of His way, the God of the universe would seek to have a relationship with mortal men and women like us!

 ## The Keeper of the Sea

*From Paul and Rebecca: July 17, 2004*

Susannah, Stephen, Rebecca, and I left for De Hanne, a town about 2 hours from here on the North Sea. The Belgian Health Service provides a facility near the beach where handicapped people can vacation. The home has all one needs: hospital beds, nurses, physical therapists, etc. The staff was kind. Susannah and Stephen stayed in a bed & breakfast just opposite—with our two dogs. It was a joy to be away together for this week.

> *While one "survives," another laughs and lives, and the waves go on, and the Lord oversees it all.*

*Rebecca's reflections to the Lord from De Hanne:*

I have returned to the seaside. As I look out over the steely gray waters of the North Sea, hear the crashing of the waves; I realized I never dreamed that I would see the ocean again. These last years I have confronted death.

At times I have struggled against it, and at others, wished to go beyond it into Father's presence. During such seasons, one does not consider the sea; one struggles just from day to day. Thoughts of soaring seagulls and children playing in the sand are far away.

*Some months ago You challenged me to "choose life." Since that choice I have discovered again: my birds, the clouds going by, the daily joy and delight of my children's laughter, my husband's love, Your Word....*

The other day when I arrived here at the boardwalk and looked out over the great expanse, the Lord spoke, "I am the Keeper of the sea." Three summers have come and gone, and while I have fought and struggled, the sea was here, unchanged. And so is life! While one "survives," another laughs and lives, and the waves go on, and the Lord oversees it all.

Some months ago You challenged me to "choose life." Since that choice I have discovered again: my birds, the clouds going by, the daily joy and delight of my children's laughter, my husband's love, Your Word penetrating my soul, and now...the sea.

Yesterday in the dining room, as we made our way to our table, I noticed a small table in the corner that was set for just one person. Soon, someone painstakingly made his way behind me in a walker. As he struggled with the table, the chair, and his walker, Paul offered to help him. He good-naturedly said, in French, of course: "Oh, no thank you. I have no one to help me at home, and I must be independent." As he settled in his chair, ready for his lunch, I couldn't help but look at him and smile. His face was etched—was it with pain? Determination? Probably both.

Later we made our way to the elevator. I was struck by the realization that no one was in a hurry. And I thought: "Of course not. If there is anything we've all learned is to be patient and to wait." It is a patience wrought in waiting.

**Waiting in His Presence**

*From Rebecca, February 7, 2005*

About a week ago, Paul left for a 3-week trip to North America. I am here with my excellent caregivers, Judy, Annie, and Jessica. What a great team we are! The morning Paul left, I felt a bit overwhelmed and blue, and called to Jessica: "I need to write. Will you please take dictation for me?" I "wrote" the following, and I share it now with you:

It was thirty years ago. We had not been long in our house on Linden Walk, which was our first real home. Early one morning I was in the kitchen and our car backed out from the driveway. My beloved was leaving on a trip and I was left at home. I was young (28 years old—Paul and I had married when we were 21.) I didn't go with Paul on this trip because of the precious little one asleep upstairs. I had always traveled with Paul, and part of why we had delayed having children was that I was torn by the thought of staying home while he traveled. Now that day had come.

I began to cry, picked up the broom and through my tears furiously began to sweep the kitchen. Then the Lord spoke. I love the ways the Lord's words come to us, simply, never to be forgotten. He said, "This is your price for My Kingdom."

---

> *"If you're at home in God and I'm at home in God, we can't be far apart."*
>
> —*George MacDonald*

---

And now today, over thirty years later, I am left at home again. This time I am bound by the limits of my own body. Just as surely as a changed lifestyle was Father's great gift to me 30 years ago, so my paralysis is His instrument and gift today. This gift is not so easy for me to understand, but I pray: "Oh Love, guard my mind in peace and quietness."

Three weeks stretch out before me. It seems so long. By His grace, I must take one day at a time, and together we will discover what good He has in store. Today I can't grab my broom and busy myself; but the blessed years have tempered me and I can wait each day with expectation to see the kindness and tasks that He has planned. My focus and my joy must not be on me but on pleasing Him.

Many years ago I read a quote by George MacDonald, the great 19th century writer, and the man C.S. Lewis called his master. He wrote to one of his children: "If you're at home in God and I'm at home in God, we can't be far apart." That is an overarching reality for me, and our family. We live our lives in Father's presence and can know closeness to those we love even in the face of geographical distance. I thank our Father that He, and His grace, is sufficient for everything we face.

CHAPTER SIX

# Knowing the Lord

*"And this is life eternal,*
*that they may know You,*
*the only true God,*
*and Jesus Christ whom*
*You have sent."*
John 17:3 (NKJV)

*"One thing I have desired of the Lord,*
*that will I seek: That I may dwell*
*in the house of the Lord*
*all the days of my life,*
*To behold the beauty of the Lord,*
*and to inquire in His temple.*
*When You said, 'Seek my face,'*
*my heart said to you,*
*'Your face, Lord, I will seek.'"*
Psalm 27:4 & 8 (NKJV)

THE GREATEST JOURNEY OF MY LIFE HAS BEEN MY journey to the Father's heart. Perhaps on October 4<sup>th</sup>, Father said, "I think Rebecca knows Me well enough that we can set out on a great adventure." My knowledge of Him had been settled through many days, hour upon hour in His presence, seeking Him.

When we meet new friends, we like them, but we don't know them. And it's possible to begin to build a relationship. We have time together, we explore each other's experiences, and we delight to learn each other's joys and sorrows. All of this evolves over time. And so it is with Father. Philippians 3:10 says the apostle Paul gave up everything, "that I might know Him..." (NKJV). The notes in one translation say, "That I might discover the wonders of His personality." I remember as a college student I read that in amazement and said, "Lord, You mean You have a personality?" And so I set out to know Him in a new way.

And now these days it would be my knowledge of Him that would enable me to navigate through the unthinkable in the midst of the unknowable. I could hold my soul steady in the One I knew loved me. Romans 8:28-29 says "...we know that to those who love God...everything that happens fits into a pattern for good..." (Phillips). Even this nightmare, as I give it to Him, He will turn it into good and use it to increase the marvelous revelation of Himself and His purpose on the earth.

## DURING ICU AND THE HOSPITAL

Immediately after the accident, October 4, 2001 – March 27, 2002

 **Caught Between Two Realms**

Everything is swirling confusion. My body is heavy, deadweight, my thoughts coming in and out—and I'm afraid. What in the world has happened? When my beloved Paul is here, it's much better—and then they make him leave me. If he could just stay. And the Lord, He's not really close. If He could just stay. But oh, we've walked together for so many years. And surely I do know that when Paul leaves me, his heart is still with me. Father is the same way. How thankful I am, Lord, that I

*Help me, Lord, to breathe again. Or let me come to be with You. I don't think I can bear to live like this. But if somehow this is what You have for me, then give me strength, and give me enough love for me to follow You...even here.*

know You so well. I don't count on my feelings, but on who You are, and You are good.

I don't understand this swirling unreality. I wish it weren't real. Perhaps it's not. But oh, the weight of my arms and legs is pressing the reality to me. Most of all, I hate the hissing of the respirator. Help me, Lord; help me, Lord, to breathe again. Or let me come to be with You. I don't think I can bear to live on like this. Everyone would be sad, but they'd be okay eventually. And if somehow this is what You have for me, then give me courage and give me strength, and give me enough love for me to follow You even here.

 ## Quiet Place Within

*From Paul, October 05, 2001*

Day two has been difficult—some good news, and some not so good. The results of the MRI showed no break in the spinal cord. That was good news. The doctors still will give us no prognosis, however. They are waiting to do the surgery on the fractured vertebrae, perhaps in another 2 or 3 days. For the children and me these are difficult days. We cannot help Rebecca because we have no way of knowing her needs. She is locked in a body that doesn't feel or move, and now cannot speak. Please pray with us that she will quickly be able to breathe on her own.

As the children and I prayed together, I knew that though I could not hear her, the Father could. And though I did not know her needs, the Father

> *"I have never known such helplessness, such dependence—or such knowledge that He will be all to her that she needs Him to be."* —Paul

does. And, though the hospital limits time I can be with her, God is always there. I prayed that Rebecca would flee the outside confines and conflicts of that precious body and run to the place in her heart where she communes with Christ and find her real home in Him. Only He can be what she needs. No matter how desperately I want to help her, only He can now.

I have never known such helplessness, such dependence—or such knowledge that He will be all to her that she needs Him to be.

The doctors assure us that this will be a long process. I trust it will be a successful one. One day this will be history, a memory. And she will be walking, active, living, and serving again.

*From Paul, December 26, 2001*

It's funny where one's mind wanders in difficult times. I was sitting in our bedroom this morning. It felt so empty without my dear Rebecca. I found myself reflecting on the emptiness of heaven after Jesus came to be among us. His birth here had to be bittersweet for the Father and those who loved His presence there in heaven. What did the angels experience when the One who had been their light stepped out of their midst? Things just weren't the same. I'm sure the Father anticipated with longing and joys those late-night encounters with His Son on the mountain; they had been together for all eternity.

Proverbs 7 speaks of the depth of their relationship. Now Jesus was down here, not "up" there. They still had wonderful fellowship—but it wasn't the same. I became more aware of Father's love and the sacrifice He made in sending Jesus. What a comfort that love is to us now.

## DURING REHAB

At Pellenburg Rehabilitation Center after the time in ICU and Hospital,
March 27, 2002 – April 11, 2003

 ### In the Secret of His Presence

Often when I come in for lunch from my morning sessions, there is mail for me from some of my dear friends.

Last week, we received a letter from Mark and Tacee Puttick. It included a wonderful picture of Winnie the Pooh. Winnie was stuck in a hole and asking: "Would you read a sustaining book, such as would help and comfort a wedged bear in great tightness?" The letter went on to quote just such a book by Frank Laubach, and a poem. One of the lines of the poem says:"How precious are the lessons which I learned at Jesus' side."

The next morning, as I prepared for the day, I meditated on those lines. I felt the Lord said: "Treat people as I would treat people." Often when the Lord gives me instruction, before I begin to

> *"Would you read a sustaining book, such as would help and comfort a wedged bear in great tightness?"*
>
> —*Winne the Pooh*

implement it, I realize He has already put someone around me who is a living example of the task He is calling me to. I began, that morning, to try to treat people like Jesus would treat them.

When I arrived at my therapy class, my young therapist began to mobilize my left hand. This is an important part of my program. It keeps my hands from becoming stiff. Before she sat down on the stool beside me, she said, "Rebecca, do you need a drink of water?" I did! She brought me back a cold drink. As she gave it to me, with such kindness and a lovely smile, I thought of Jesus' words about giving a drink of water in His name.

Next, she lovingly (I don't know how else to describe it) took my hand and began to work. She held each joint, sometimes for as long as several minutes. I finally said: "Miriella, why do you hold each joint for such a long time?" "Oh," she said, "I have to hold it until it releases. I can feel it relax after time."

I thought of Jesus when He said: "Come to me… and I will give you rest" (Matthew 11:28, NIV). Sometimes we feel like He's holding on to us so tightly for such a longtime, and we don't understand. But He feels the release, and knows what will bring real rest. Here is the poem, "In the Secret of His Presence," which I received this week, written by Helen L. Goreh in 1883:

*In the secret of His presence by*
*How my soul delights to hide!*
*Oh, how precious are the lessons*
*Which I learn at Jesus' side!*
*Earthly cares can never vex me,*
*Neither trials lay me low;*
*For when Satan comes to tempt me,*
*To the secret place I go.*

*When my soul is faint and thirsty,*
*'Neath the shadow of His wing*
*There is cool and pleasant shelter,*
*And a fresh and crystal spring;*
*And my Savior rests beside me,*
*As we hold communion sweet:*
*If I tried, I could not utter*
*What He says when thus we meet.*

**Our Adventure Together to the Father**

A new translation of the New Testament had recently been done into Flemish; some weeks ago I asked Paul to get several for me to give to people. On the last day of work for Natalie, a nursing student at Pellenburg, I gave one to her. I pointed her to Matthew 11:28-30, "Come to me, all you who are weary and burdened…" (NIV). She immediately went off by herself with her New Testament, only to come back in 15 minutes with tears streaming down her face. She said: "How did you know what I needed? God has spoken to me!" I just said: "Natalie, go to Jesus and He will lead you to the Father." What a daily adventure we are all having together; as we pray, Jesus is leading. I still have three more New Testaments. Won't it be fun to see who they are for?

 **Teach Me to Listen**

"Lord, teach me to listen." This prayer was not a surprise to me. It seems the Lord had been calling me to listen to Him for thirty years. An important part of any relationship is communicating with one another. To communicate we must listen to each other as well as talk. One of Amy Carmichael's poems reflects this truth:

> *What do I know of listening?*
> *O my Father,*
> *Teach me in silence*
> *of the soul to gather*
> *Those thoughts of Thine that,*
> *deep within me flowing,*
> *Like the currents of a river,*
> *guide my going.*

I'm grateful the Lord has given me a focus to begin these days. That focus is to seek Him, fling my will, my all, into the daily climb, and allow His thoughts to daily "guide my going."

## AT HOME

Home to stay, April 11, 2003

 ### Change is Necessary

*From Rebecca, March 29, 2004*

One of the main things I wanted to speak with the doctor about was the recent change I've felt, that of increased numbness. I was encouraged by his report, and know now that I will have variations in sensation and spasticity.

Several weeks ago, I felt upset when I began to experience a new numbness on the left side. The next morning I went before the Lord and cried out to Him: "Don't tell me there will be something else. I don't know if I can bear it." And He quietly reminded me: "Change is necessary for you."

George MacDonald, the Scottish writer and poet of the 19th and early 20th centuries, said: "How changed must the human soul be to fellowship with the God of the universe!" Remembering that, I began to thank Him that even in this change, He would adjust my soul to be able to know Him better.

On the same morning, I found an excerpt by Jean-Pierre de Caussade (1675-1751), a French Jesuit priest.

*"God's order and His divine will is the life*
*of all souls who either seek or obey it. In*
*whatever way this divine will may benefit the*
*mind, it nourishes the soul. These blessed*
*results are not produced by any particular*
*circumstance, but by what God ordains for the*

*present moment. What was best a moment ago*
*is so no longer, because it is removed from the*
*divine will which has passed on to be changed*
*to form the duty to the next. And it is that*
*duty, whatever that may be, that is now most*
*sanctifying for the soul."*

I wept as I read to realize once again how faithful Father is to speak to me. It is a lovely reality that when change comes, it will always turn out for our growth in Him—enabling us to more fully fellowship with Him. "Father, help us remember this in the little changes as well as the big ones."

 **There Is a Redeemer**

*From Rebecca, January 23, 2005*

Last night I was unable to sleep. I kept singing, over and over, "There is a Redeemer, Jesus, God's own Son; precious Lamb of God, Messiah, Holy One." I struggled to stop singing, and tried to

*His mother rushed to help*
*Him. Jesus said: "No, I*
*must do this. I'm making*
*all things new."*

sleep. Surely I needed my rest. Suddenly I realized the Holy Spirit was singing in me, and the Lord was calling me to a time with Him. I sang and sang and sang, meditating on our Redeemer.

One of my favorite parts of the movie *The Passion* was the poignant line as Jesus fell under the weight of the cross on the way to Golgotha, and His mother rushed to help Him. He said: "No, I must do this. I'm making all things new." Oh, how many times I've needed a Redeemer, One to make my situation new.

This past week I've been reading in John 4 where Jesus met the

Samaritan woman at the well. What a mess her life was! How desperately she needed a Redeemer! The incredible thing to me was that Jesus used all the bad things in her life, and made good of them. Because of her "position" in the village, everyone knew her. She knew the men, who in that culture were the leaders. Later in the chapter it says that she went back and told all the men about what had happened to her. Jesus redeemed the sinful life—He made good out of her past, using even it for His glory and the advancement of His Kingdom. It says that many believed because of her words. Then Jesus stayed on in the village, and many more believed because of His own words. This "sinful woman" had become an evangelist. Such a Redeemer!

> *Jesus met the Samaritan woman at the well. What a mess her life was! Jesus used all the bad things in her life, and made good of them.*

I thought of our own state of affairs. In the natural, what a mess! But Jesus is a Redeemer. I've been struck this week with the reality that, because of all we've been through, Father seems to be making a platform from which we can share His goodness and His love. It is amazing to me to realize that this quadriplegic is becoming an evangelist. Such a Redeemer!

##  I Have Chased You Down to Bless You

*From Rebecca, January 28, 2006*

Nineteen years ago, at the age of 41, we discovered I was pregnant. My pregnancy with Phillip three years earlier had been complicated; I spent seven months in bed. When Phillip was born, a beautiful healthy baby boy, we were thrilled, and knew that every moment of bed rest had been worth the price. But, the thought of doing it again was overwhelming.

Now I found myself back in bed, once again waiting for a new baby. I had so many emotions. In the swirl the Lord spoke to me and said: "I have chased you down to bless you." How could we ever say what a blessing and joy Stephen is to us today?

I was reminded of this last week when I read a definition of "bless" in my Bible. From God's side, He is the blesser, the One who gives the capacity for living a full, rich life.

We have seen so often that just before a season of blessing there is a "moment" of pain or stretching. Does it prepare us to be able to receive God's blessing?

I've experienced this pattern in my own life! Often I will have a period of weakness just before an event to which I have been looking with excitement! This past week we had been planning for the whole family to go to see the play *Oliver*. The night before, I didn't sleep well. My body does not regulate temperature normally. I can become hot or cold. These patterns interrupt my sleep, and sometimes even involve calling one of my caregivers to turn up the heat or take blankets off.

*There can be many kinds of stretching experiences. Sometimes the Lord asks us to go a little further, lay down something precious, forgive, or "let go." Each of these can be the pathway of opening ourselves to Him for Him to give us the ability to receive His blessing.*

Friday night was such a night. As Saturday dawned, I felt weary and unsure that I would be able to go to the play. I've learned to recognize this pattern, and press through as much as I am able. So I continued Saturday. The closer we got to the theater, the stronger I felt. When we arrived I thought: "I can do this."

It was a delightful afternoon. I enjoyed it to the fullest even though I was in the wheelchair for more than 5 hours. Our whole family shared this special time together. We came home and sat around the dinner table, talking of the joy of this occasion.

There can be many kinds of stretching experiences. Sometimes the Lord asks us to go a little further, lay down something precious, forgive, or "let go." Each of these can be the pathway of opening ourselves to Him for Him to give us the ability to receive His blessing.

> *He walked away from the Master, and from being enlarged enough to have the capacity to receive the blessing of God.*

A rich young ruler came to Jesus. He was a young man who seemed to have all the world could give— and yet he came seeking. The Scripture says that Jesus loved him. I've always been amazed to think of what a relationship with Jesus he could have had. Jesus put His finger on the center of that in his life, which kept him from receiving the fullness of what God had for him. He turned away "sad." He walked away from the Master, and from being enlarged enough to have the capacity to receive the blessing of God. Imagine what Jesus could have given him! That's what He has for us today. I want to be able to open myself to let Father give me the capacity to be blessed, as is in His heart.

##  The Living Reality of Being United with Jesus

*From Paul, March 14, 2007*

I don't usually share my spiritual musings in *Rebecca's Journey*, but one verse in Philippians has been nourishing for me lately. Philippians 2:1: "If you have any encouragement from being united with Christ..." (NIV). I've meditated on this for days. What deep, broad, and substantive encouragement we have from being united with Jesus! And it's not the *idea* that is encouraging, but the living *reality* of being united with Jesus!

The One who loves us and gave Himself for us, lives in us by His Spirit.

He's not faraway waiting to be called to action on our behalf. He's closer than our breath. Courage, heart, confidence, endurance, strength, and anticipation of His good purpose all emerge inside us from His life in us.

More importantly this union gives us opportunity for deep fellowship with Him, as He progressively integrates our lives with Himself. It's above and beyond what we could have imagined. And there's more to come! Great encouragement! ✲

# Picture Gallery

We are swooping in...

10/2008

THE PETRIE FAMILY (about 1988)
Paul and Rebecca with Matthew, Susannah, Phillip, and Stephen

Paul and Rebecca just before the accident (August, 2001)

Paul and Rebecca (2005)

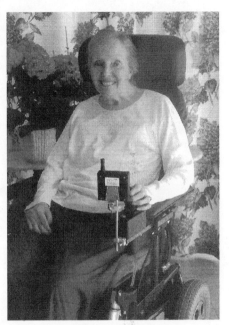

Rebecca's sister, Judy, with Laura
Christensen, one of Rebecca's
dearest friends.

Rebecca at home

Paul and Rebecca

Hospitality is still an important part of Paul and Rebecca's lives

Rebecca with some of her wonderful caregivers

(From left to right): Matthew and Stephanie, Susannah,
Josie and Phillip, and Stephen

Susannah and Rebecca                Paul with Gabriella

CHAPTER SEVEN

## Tapestry of Relationships

*"My command is this: Love each other
as I have loved you. Greater love has no
one than this, that he lay down his life
for his friends."*
John 15:12 (NIV)

*"...I tell you the truth, whatever you
did for one of the least of these
brothers of mine, you did for me."*
Matthew 25:40 (NIV)

ON THE MORNING THAT I FELL, I HAD BEEN TEACHING a group of women, praying together and sharing with them from Ephesians 2. In *The Message* it reads, "Now God has us where He wants us...to shower grace and kindness upon us..." I went immediately from teaching those verses, fell, and broke my neck. "Now, Lord, how can this be kindness and grace?" Oh, He was about to show me the miracle of how He turns all into good.

The picture that I have is of a long chain of faithful faces. It is unbroken, one after the other. The first Christmas after I fell in October, I was in ICU. There was a knock on the door of Room 13. I lay with my tubes and monitors. In came the smiling face of my dear friend Laura Christensen, with a warm "Merry Christmas! We have a special gift for you from the hundreds of people who love you and are praying for you." In her arms she was carrying a most beautiful, huge patchwork quilt. I was amazed. Laura

*The patchwork quilt came from Europe, America, Africa, and Assia. Both sides were covered with blessings, Scriptures, and prayers. Laura covered me with it and said, "You rest here now under the prayers and love of your friends."*

had sent patches to dozens of our friends. They returned them by mail and by fax—from places where there was no mail. They came from Europe, America, Africa, and Asia. Both sides were covered with blessings, Scriptures, and prayers. She covered me over with it, and said, "You rest here now under the prayers and love of your friends."

Our life has been built on relationships, the faithful joining and love of one brother and sister to another, under our Father's care and oversight. Our first calling is to Him, and then to one another. This gift of love, the quilt and the women who contributed to it, expressed beautifully all that we had given our life to.

## DURING ICU AND THE HOSPITAL

Immediately after the accident, October 4, 2001 – March 27, 2002

 **Surrounded by Love**

As the days and weeks stretched into months, and Room 13 did become my home, I found myself "showered with the kindness" the Lord had promised in Ephesians chapter two. Paul had determined that I would not be alone and so he arranged that any time my family could not be with me, a friend would come. Thus began the parade of friends to my

> *Thus began the parade of friends to my bedside, a faithful expression of their love that would last as long as I was there.*

bedside, a faithful expression of their love that would last as long as I was there. The doctors and nurses in ICU had to be the best and kindest that anyone could have. As with my friends, so it was with my medical support: it was just the beginning of marvelous care that I would constantly receive. He proved faithful to His Word, even when I could not sense His presence directly.

 **"You Are the Sun Here"**

*From Denise Baines, one of our British friends and caregivers*

The doctor who is head of the ICU came to see Rebecca. After examining her, he sat down and looking directly at her said in French, "You always have such a beautiful smile." Rebecca just smiled! Then he looked more intently at her. "You are one of the most seriously ill patients in the ICU, but 'vous etes le soleil ici' — 'you are the sun here.'"

Rebecca mouthed in French, "Thank you very much; that's very kind."

But the doctor insisted: "I'm not saying this to be kind. I am saying it because it is the truth. You are really the sun here." He looked at me for support, and I agreed with him that this was true. He continued: "It must be difficult for you, I know it must. But, really, you are the sun here." He spoke slowly and with great emphasis, brushing away her thanks. Then he further insisted: "It's not just me who says this; other people here are saying the same." I had the impression he did not want to leave, and perhaps would have liked to know more about this incredible woman. He insisted a few more times and finally left. Wow.

*"In the early weeks I went to my e-mail like a starving man, and devoured the encouragement, faith, comfort, Scripture, and perspective sent by many of you. Those notes were like sustaining food—and all saved for a time when I can read them to Rebecca."*

—*Paul*

 **Life is Relationships**

*From Paul, October 24, 2001*

What I would give to take this from her! But One who loves her more than I do is overseeing our way. The Lord often reminds me that life doesn't consist of the things we have—even mobility. Life's substance is in our relationships—first with Him, then with one another. In this definition, life is full and rich for my beloved. And it will be these relationships that sustain her.

 **The Body of Christ**

*From Paul, December 14, 2001*

The staff just took Rebecca to the operating "theater," as they call it here. I'm waiting in her room. She was so thankful to know that you are carrying her in prayer. She said: "I feel like I am at the end. And that is not a bad thing. Thank You, Lord, that I am at the end." I said that when we are at our end God is not at His. His mercies never fail. Yesterday marked 10 weeks here in ICU. She was peaceful about the procedure, but nervous about what she will experience when she comes out of the anesthetic. It was in this context that she mentioned her gratitude for your prayer.

I was thinking today about the Body of Christ. From the beginning of this ordeal we have been so strengthened by you, the Lord's people. In the early weeks I went to my e-mail like a starving man, and devoured the encouragement, faith, comfort, Scripture, and perspective sent by many of you. Those notes were like sustaining food—and are all saved for a time when I can read them to Rebecca. Then in the more recent weeks your notes and insights, your encouragement and love, have meant a tremendous amount to Rebecca. I've printed them out daily and brought them in to read to her. They are in a folder to be edited later—so full of insight, faith, and up building.

In prayer, too, we've so desperately needed others bearing the burden with us. I said to a friend recently that I can carry the daily prayer for the things that face us. But others need to carry the prayer for the future. I haven't the spiritual/emotional energy for that—let alone the time. But I know God has called others to carry that kind of intercession for us. There is reality in this "bearing one another's burdens."

## DURING REHAB

At Pellenburg Rehabilitation Center after the time in ICU and Hospital,
March 27, 2002 – April 11, 2003

 **Forgiveness**

They say in rehabilitation that even in the best weeks we will have some bad moments. Wednesday morning was one of those bad moments. It began when a new student nurse was assigned to give me my bath. Either she could not hear me or she could not understand my English. She kept shouting: "What?" Since we are a family who says, "Pardon?" I am afraid that alone put us off to a bad start. It was downhill from there. I became irritable and began fussing at her. When she left, I felt so badly, that I called her back, apologized for my attitude, and asked her to forgive me. This is the third time I have had to do this with a nurse. From their response, I do not think it is something they are used to. In all three situations, it has resulted in our being close and developing a friendship. This little student nurse was no exception.

It reminded me of the value of the Lord's admonitions to forgive, and to ask forgiveness. I realized that when I say: "I'm sorry; would you please forgive me?" it is taking the humble place, saying I was wrong. Andrew Murray wrote that humility is the foundation for all other virtues. I think one of the greatest ways humility is expressed is to ask for forgiveness. Humility draws God's grace to us and to our circumstances.

---

*Then one morning it swept over me that He loved me. With that came such overwhelming love for Him. Then I remembered: "You love me because I first loved you." I cannot make myself love God.*

---

###  The Depths of His Love

I have a small sign on my bulletin board that was written by an 11-year-old friend. It says simply, "I love you." When it came, I thought it was a sweet gesture, and had it put up. Several days later, when I woke in the morning and my eyes fell on it, the Lord spoke: "I love you!" I was taken back to the early days in the ICU. I remembered being semi-conscious, heavily drugged, and with a vague awareness that He was calling me to learn to love Him more. In the days and weeks that followed, I began to "work at" consciously loving Him. Then one morning it swept over me that He loved *me*. With that came such an overwhelming love for Him. Then I remembered: "You love me because I first loved you." I cannot make myself love God.

So, here I am again, fifteen months later, realizing anew the God of the universe loves me. He loves me through all those who know and love me, and their constant care and prayer. I don't understand it, but it brings out of my heart such a love for Him. It makes me feel so humbled that many are still standing with us. I weep again as I say this. I know that it can only be His love that binds us, and makes us one. It is a powerful way to start the New Year, as members of His body, in weakness and strength, around the world, praying for one another.

 ## Seeking the Lord in the Morning

We've had wonderful e-mails, letters, and cards from many—so encouraging and strengthening. During this time I did not know how to have my devotional time, since I couldn't write in my journal or read my Bible. Well, I've come up with a new way. When a letter or card touches me in a special way, I have it put in the outside pocket of a beautiful little bag that a friend made for me. It hangs on my bed. In the mornings, after I take my 8:00 medication, the nurses say, "Do you want your cards?" Then they stack the notes and cards on my chest, go out, and close the door. Sometimes it is quite a process, because I only have one good hand, and it is not very agile. So between my left hand and my teeth, I turn the cards, find the scriptures or paragraphs, and the

> *Between my left hand and my teeth, I turn the cards, find the Scriptures or paragraphs, and the Lord touches and encourages me for the day.*

Lord touches and encourages me for the day. It is a wonderful, living word.

I was blessed last week when Mieka, one of my favorite nurses, told me as she was leaving for vacation, "Rebecca, I have something for you before I leave." She gave me a card and said, "This is to put in your little bag and to read in the morning." It was a beautiful card, chosen carefully just for me. This showed me the nurses and my medical support team understood the significance of my quiet moments alone with Father in the morning. Since then, Mieka has become a dear and precious friend.

*"Sunday brunch was Rebecca's first meal at the table in over 14 months. We wheeled her chair to a beautifully decorated Christmas table, looking out over the garden. Stephen fixed omelets and other goodies."* —Paul

 **The Heart of Life— Relationships**

From Paul, December 10, 2002

It's Monday afternoon, and I'm at the hospital. We had a wonderful 30 hours at home with Rebecca over the weekend. We began decorating for Christmas. Stephen was the motor behind this, with Rebecca giving suggestions from her bed, while being surrounded by boxes of decorations and pine boughs. Sunday brunch was Rebecca's first meal at the table in over 14 months. We wheeled her chair to a beautifully decorated Christmas table, looking out over the garden. Stephen fixed omelets and other goodies. She says she's not ready for a fancy restaurant yet, but it is another real step forward. The heart of life and its joy is in our relationship with Him and one another. Love fills life in such a satisfying way.

 **Christmas at Home**

From Paul, January 03, 2003

On Christmas Eve, Susannah, Phillip, Stephen, and I picked Rebecca up from the hospital and brought her home for 9 days. The house was a

Christmas wonderland, and Rebecca's bed was in the middle of it all. Matt and Stephanie arrived for our family Christmas celebration. And celebration it was! The days flowed from one delightful encounter to another, all enrobed in His presence. Everyone worked together as a team, each making his or her contribution (many hands make light work). Then yesterday we took her back to Pellenberg. Knowing that in just a few weeks she will begin coming home every weekend mitigated our sadness, and in a few months she will be home for good.

 ## Integrating Our Life Together

*From Paul, February 20, 2003*

One extra prayer request: For the past 37 years, Rebecca and I have created our life together, partnering not only in raising our children, but in all that we've done and initiated. We've worked and traveled together, and our life

---

*"My desire and commitment is that the life ahead of us will proceed out of our relationship just as the life behind us has. We frankly don't know how to do this."—Paul*

---

has unfolded out of our relationship and communication. Rebecca's present limitations create a new situation. My desire and commitment is that the life ahead of us will proceed out of our relationship just as the life behind us has. We frankly don't know how to do this. Rebecca will be moving home in about 6 weeks. We're making the preparations for that now. I don't want to go about my life and just "visit" her regularly in her room. We need wisdom and insight to know how to create our future together.

> *"For the greater part of my life, her bright, dancing, hazel eyes have been a light in my life, shining with laughter and compassion. It is challenging to daily see quiet, courageous suffering in those lovely eyes."* —Paul

## DURING LONDON SURGERIES

The London surgeries took place during the time in rehab,

July 11, 2002 – August 2, 2002

 **Standing Together**

*From Paul, July 02, 2002*

Facing these surgeries is a bit daunting to me. I have some niggling fear. I'm glad David said, "...I will fear no evil, for you are with me..." (Psalm 23:4, NIV). Rebecca's overall condition is not as good as it has been, and the pressure on the spinal column by the first vertebrae is causing decreased sensitivity and movement.

Rebecca and I met when we were eighteen years old, were engaged at nineteen, and married at twenty-one. We have grown up together. Next month we will celebrate our thirty-sixth wedding anniversary. For the greater part of my life her bright, dancing, hazel eyes have been a light in my life, shining with laughter and compassion. It is challenging to daily see quiet, courageous suffering in those lovely eyes.

## AT HOME

Home to stay, April 11, 2003

 **A Band of Brothers and Sisters**

This morning I'm holding in my hand two lists. One is of many of you who were part of last week's prayer vigil. The second is the list of those who, like me, are suffering from injuries and disease that can only be healed by a divine touch. As I hold the two lists I can only weep. I keep hearing in my mind the words from Shakespeare's "Henry V" where King Henry spoke to his men just before a decisive battle saying: "We few, we happy few, we band of brothers; for he today that sheds his blood with me shall be my brother" (Henry V, Act 4, Scene 3).

Surely we stand and fight together, a band of brothers and sisters, bound not by the love of a nation, but by the love of the Lord Jesus and His Kingdom.

I'm reminded of a word the Lord spoke to me: "You don't understand what I'm doing. It is far beyond your ability to understand. But one day it will be clear." Our Brotherhood/Sisterhood, forged in these hours through our pain—completing the sufferings of Christ—is a bond different and broader than we've known before or can understand.

> *"We few, we happy few, we band of brothers; for he today that sheds his blood with me shall be my brother."*
>
> *(Henry V, Act 4, Scene 3)*

Jesus said in Matthew 25:40, "...I tell you the truth, whatever you did for one of the least of these brothers of mine, you did for me" (NIV). I'm so thankful for the faithfulness of so many to pray and support us because, in doing so, His Body on the earth has been strengthened. What a fine band of friends we have, standing together in these times. What a lovely expression of Jesus' life!

 **First Visits Home**

*From Paul, November 18, 2002*

Once more it is Sunday afternoon. We're back at Pellenberg. Rebecca is napping, regaining strength after yesterday's adventure.

The ambulance pulled up at our home right at 11:00. Stephanie and Matt had arrived earlier from Germany for the day with their little dog, Lew. Thirteen months ago, when Rebecca left us, the house had been under construction. Yesterday she entered what was to be her "new" home. After some tears, shed by all of us, we pushed her bed from the dining/living room into the kitchen, which she had designed but had never seen. Everything was a delight. Her great compliment to me: "You've decorated it just the way I would have." (That had been my goal.) You can imagine the three dogs created a small riot. Hope, our 15-year old little mutt, soon settled herself on Rebecca's bed, where she spent the rest of the day.

Stephen had lit the fire, and then cooked Judy's birthday lunch. About 2:30 the nurse arrived for her duties. After a nap, we shared together around the fire and Judy opened her gifts as the afternoon sped away. Seven o'clock came all too quickly. And again, tears at her departure. What a lovely day—one that glows in all our memories!

##  Weaving the Tapestry One Person at a Time

*From Rebecca, April 20, 2004*

We are blessed to be surrounded and carried as we are by your love and prayer. I want to report that after the day of prayer on my birthday, April 4, we have seen some definite progress. From that day, my spasticity has been noticeably less. And I am beginning to have movement in my right hip joint. Just today, my physical therapist said: "It's moving! This is just how the left leg began almost a year ago." This is caused by nerve re-enervation. We are 2½ years after the accident, and such a change as this is remarkable.

> *"When your friends pray, you just get stronger and stronger..."*
> —Rebecca's physical therapist

Today I would like to tell you about my physical therapist. Last week she bubbled into my room (every morning she comes like a ray of sunshine—such an encourager). "Today is our one year anniversary," she said. "We have been working together for a year." About a week before my birthday she had said to me, "You are just like

Lazare." "Lazare?" I thought, "Who in the world is Lazare?" She continued, "You know him. He's the guy who was dead and Jesus called him forth out of the grave. His friends said that he was going to stink! But Jesus raised him from the dead." Then she went on, "When your friends pray, you just get stronger and stronger."

Then came my birthday, and I told her many of my friends were going to pray again. She laughed. The following week, after the prayer, we experienced the much-diminished spasticity that I mentioned earlier. "This prayer thing really works," she exclaimed. "You tell your friends to keep praying and that your physical therapist said 'Thank You.'" Then she said, "You, me, and God are making quite a team."

### From Paul

When our physical therapist first came to us she was openly skeptical towards religion. One of the joys of the last years has been to see the impact of faith on those who serve Rebecca—and the process continues.

 **Committed to the Highest Good**

### From Paul, August 16, 2006

Rebecca and I are about to celebrate our 40th wedding anniversary. Susannah, representing our children, asked if Rebecca and I could write some of the significant elements and experiences in our 40 years of marriage. Our kids feel that we have a great relationship—Rebecca and I do, too! It is the result of Jesus' leadership though the years.

I met Rebecca (Becky Kunkle then) in 1964. We were in our first year of university. At the time I wasn't looking for a wife, but when I first saw her, I knew that I would marry her. That moment is imprinted in my mind: she was seated, wearing a cream blouse with a flowing bow at the neck, black skirt, and pointed black high heeled shoes. Her hands were folded over her crossed knees, her head raised, with a bouffant 60's hairstyle. I was stunned! She looked like an angel.

With my typical reserve I walked directly over to her and introduced myself, then walked her back to her dorm. Let me say here that she hadn't had the epiphany which I experienced on first seeing her. It took me a while to convince her to marry me. But one of the things that got both our attention early was that we shared a deep commitment to Jesus, and a sense of destiny. We each knew that He had a purpose for our lives.

We began our journey together during those days, focused on following Him, seeking to know His plan, His ideas, His preferences. (We fought a lot too!)

As we approached our wedding day, August 27, 1966, we understood little about a "Biblical marriage." There weren't teachings or conferences on marriage in those days (at least none that we knew of). We knew only one thing clearly as we said "I Do!"

Our commitment on that day was first to Him, of course. But second, Rebecca and I committed ourselves "to the others' highest good at our own expense." Those were the words we used, and they represented our deepest understanding of relationship at the time.

> *"Our conflicts became deep and painful, but that first decision to be committed to the other person's highest good at our own expense was our guiding principle."*
>
> —Paul

As our life together continued, our conflicts became deep and painful, but that first decision to be committed to the other person's highest good at our own expense was the guiding principle. Of course, we had a Guiding Person, too, who was faithful to help us implement our commitment.

##  A Solid Bulwark

*From Rebecca, August 25, 2006*

When we first married, it was difficult. We loved each other deeply, but how do we live together as God would have us? I am a strong woman and Paul is stronger yet. Now that is a formula for fireworks, as you can well imagine.

In about our sixth year, we began to hear and understand what the Scripture had to say about marriage and we realized it was a partnership with an authority structure forged in love, respect, and faith. As Paul was set over our home to lead us in love, I was to follow him in faith. Together we would form a solid bulwark to protect our children and fulfill the purpose and destiny that God had for us together.

Now for the working out of this! Could it be that it has taken forty years and we're still in the process? But what a lovely process!

I remember once when Matthew and Susannah were little and I was so tired. Paul had just returned from a trip. He lovingly suggested that he would take the children to church and I could rest at home. They all left and the house was deliciously quiet—but a mess. I began to pick up toys and straighten. I did the dishes and finally went upstairs to rest. Coming into our room, there was Paul's suitcase—still not unpacked. I hung up the shirts, very frustrated. As I threw his shoes into the back of closet the Lord spoke to me, "It's a privilege to serve a man of God."

> *"Could it be that it has taken forty years and we're still in the process? But what a lovely process!"*

It was one of those times when the Lord "turned the prism." Suddenly, I saw my husband in a new light, seeing him as God sees him. From my human perspective, I often saw Paul as my husband whom I loved but who often was the source of pain and struggle. I had not yet learned to look at my own sin first, so I laid the blame for most things on him. However, through the Lord's eyes, he was a man of God. Though he was not perfect, he was called and anointed to lead our home and me.

Ephesians 5 says that we, as women, are to respect our husbands. In retrospect, this was a critical point in our walk together. There are often many things that cloud our vision of one another. My own selfishness and pride kept me from seeing Paul from God's perspective. By turning my prism to see Paul more clearly, I found a deeper respect for him.

I think today of those of you who might be in a difficult marriage. Even in the middle of that, let the Lord "turn the prism" for you, so you might see your husband through His eyes. I love what Elizabeth Elliot wrote to a young woman who was in a painful marriage, "Leave with God what only God can change; only God can change the hearts of men."

Through the years, we've seen that in the most difficult circumstances, He is able to lead us through to ever-deeper oneness in Him.

##  Death in Us, Life in Others

*From Rebecca, November 10, 2006*

Recently, a friend gave me a notepad with a scripture from 3 John 4 saying, "I have no greater joy than to hear that my children are walking in the truth" (NIV).

Through the years, God has called Paul and me to labor in the lives of our own children and many young adults. At times I have felt the cost of having so many people in our home. At other times there have been difficulties, relational and interpersonal. Whatever God calls us to "do," there will be moments of cost. The apostle Paul says in 2 Corinthians 4:11-12: "For we who live are always delivered to death for Jesus' sake, that the life of Jesus also may be manifested in our mortal flesh. So then death is working in us, but life in you" (NKJV).

This is the process of "death" in us that brings life to others. Whatever God calls us to do, we can be sure

> *"For we who live are always delivered to death for Jesus' sake, that the life of Jesus also may be manifested in our mortal flesh. So then death is working in us, but life in you."*
>
> *(2 Corinthians 4:11-12 NKJV)*

in the difficult moments that He is working and that Jesus' light is being formed in us to be reflected to those around.

Often the process that God calls us to is costly. But whatever it is, we can be sure that He is working, and that Jesus' life is being formed in us. He wants to reveal Himself. When we feel the pain and are aware of the price, we must wait on Him and the fruit will come: life for others. ✳

CHAPTER EIGHT

# *Peace*

---

*"Peace I leave with you; my peace I give you, I do not give to you as the world gives. Do not let your hearts be troubled and do not be afraid."*

John 14:27 (NIV)

*"Do not be anxious about anything, but in everything, by prayer and petition, with thanksgiving, present your requests to God. And the peace of God, which transcends all understanding, will guard your hearts and your minds in Christ Jesus."*

Philippians 4:6 (NIV)

*"Do not fret — it only causes harm."*

Psalm 37:8 (NKJV)

"I JUST CAN'T DO IT. IT'S JUST TOO MUCH FOR ME." Often this was my response when Paul and I would plan our schedule for the week. Our life was busy and often so full of appointments, responsibilities, and our dear friends that I felt overwhelmed. Peace was far from me.

> *One day Paul said to me, "Rebecca, you've got to approach your life with faith and not fear."*

One day Paul said to me, "Rebecca, you've got to approach your life with faith and not fear." The Psalmist says, "...For my expectation is from Him..." (Psalm 62:5, NKJV). As I prayed about these perspectives, the Lord gave me the picture of reaching into the heavens and grabbing hold of Him for all that I needed to meet each situation. In the gospels, Jesus said that he is our peace. As we reach toward Jesus into the heavenlies our focus and our life turn toward Him, and He becomes all that we need.

Now in this desperate time in our lives, I would be able to do nothing in my weakness but reach into the heavenlies toward the One who is my peace. In some inexplicable way, His peace set guard over my heart. There were moments, when I was facing painful examinations or the news that once again something had gone wrong, that turmoil would flood in. In the swirling confusion of the moment Paul would remind me, "He is our peace."

In 1 Thessalonians 5:18, the apostle Paul cautions us, "In everything give thanks; for this is the will of God in Christ Jesus for you" (NKJV). "Lord, I can't struggle for peace. I can't make myself peaceful. I reach toward You. I thank You, Lord, for this situation." And once again His peace would flood my soul.

## DURING ICU AND THE HOSPITAL

Immediately after the accident, October 4, 2001 – March 27, 2002

 **His Peace Was Keeping Me**

Jesus said in John 14:27, "Peace I leave with you; my peace I give you..." (NIV). And that was what I experienced. As I lay in the swirl of those early days, I was uncertain about what was happening and what had happened. But somehow, looking back, there was an overriding tranquility, an overriding peace. I didn't manufacture or struggle for this peace, but in a broken state, my soul found its rest in Him. He was the One where I found my home.

I believe this came from years of walking with the Lord. We aren't suddenly able to know Him in a crisis. But our journeys before the crisis prepare us to discover the Lord in the crisis! In this greatest crisis of my life, all that had gone before ushered me into God's peace. In these days, His peace carried me. Was it from day to day? I don't know. It all ran together. In the overriding sense of His peace, He said, "It's about my love—It's about my love." And with that sure foundation, His peace garrisoned my soul.

 ## Prince of Peace

*From Paul, October 19, 2001*

Many years ago, the Lord showed me the only time I could know Him was *now*. I can anticipate meeting Him tomorrow. I can remember meeting Him yesterday. But the only time I can encounter Him is at this present moment. I, and we, have had to live moment by moment, where He and His help are. Thoughts of the past were painful. Thinking of the future can be torturous. But there is grace and peace for each moment, for each challenge, because He is there to strengthen. As the Prince of Peace, He really does give peace in the middle of dreadful conditions. It does not make sense—it passes understanding. It

> *"Many years ago, the Lord showed me the only time I could know Him was **now**. I can anticipate meeting Him tomorrow. I can remember Him yesterday. But the only time I can encounter Him is at this present moment."*
>
> —Paul

is peace that the circumstances cannot provide, and that the world cannot take away.

##  Resting in His Peace

*From Susannah, October 29, 2001*

His faithful care sustains! An overwhelming thought is how amazing Mom is. We have always known it. I told her that she is outdoing even herself. Even on the hardest of days, her spirit stays on Jesus. I have continuously sung "Turn Your Eyes upon Jesus" to her and to myself. In some of those darkest hours she would say "I am OK when I see His face."

This is not a quick or easily-won victory for her to remain in a place of peace, but she does. His presence indeed sustains us. The Holy Spirit, as token of the next world of infinite peace and strength, invades our time and space in that hospital room and invades our spirits, and there is quietness of heart.

##  Fret Not Thyself

> *"The nurses were almost as traumatized as Rebecca. They care for her, and her pain is hard for them to bear."*
>
> *—Paul*

*From Paul, January 08, 2002*

It's about 4:15 a.m. I've been up for a couple of hours, thinking, praying, "leaning." We are "inhabiting the interim," living with irresolution for the moment. Rebecca has been undergoing another series of exams, and the doctors are still undecided about what they will do next. Tomorrow will be 14 weeks since the accident, 14 weeks in Intensive Care.

The day before yesterday, Rebecca had another painful exam. I won't describe it but she said it was "torture." The nurses were almost as traumatized as Rebecca. One had to leave the room during the procedure. They care for her, and her pain was hard for them to bear. The nurses' care means so much to her.

After all of this, we read one of Amy Carmichael's poems. It caused us to reflect and be thankful. She "said" (mouthing the words), "I'm surrounded by kindness," and "He has never failed us yet." He never changes, so our hope and faith are secure. Here is the poem that touched us, "Fret Not Thyself."

*Far in the future lieth a fear;*
*Like a long, low, mist of gray,*
*Gathering to fall in dreary rain;*
*Thus doth thy heart within thee complain.*
*And even now thou art afraid,*
*For round thy dwelling*
*The flying winds are ever telling*
*Of the fear that lieth gray,*
*Like a gloom of brooding mist upon the way.*
*But The Lord is always kind;*
*Be not blind, be not blind*
*To the shining of His face,*
*To the comforts of His grace.*
*Hath He ever failed thee yet?*
*Never, never. Wherefore fret?*

*O fret not thyself, nor let*
*Thy heart be troubled,*
*Neither let it be afraid.*

*Near, by thy footfall, springeth a joy,*
*Like a new-blown little flower,*
*Growing for thee, to make thee glad.*
*Let thy countenance be no more sad,*
*But wake the voice of joy and health*
*Within thy dwelling,*
*And let thy tongue be ever telling,*
*Not of fear that lieth gray,*
*But of little flowers beside the way.*

*For the Lord is always kind,*
*Be not blind, be not blind*
*To the shining of His face,*
*To the comforts of His grace.*
*He hath never failed thee yet.*
*Never will His love forget.*
*O fret not thyself, nor let*
*Thy heart be troubled,*
*Neither let it be afraid.*

### ❀ Leaning on Him

*From Paul, January 23, 2002*

These last weeks have been challenging ones. Both of us have had periods of deep discouragement. At times I've felt that I was walking on a knife's edge, trying to keep my balance. We've just had to lean on Him.

Some mornings as I woke, that "fear that lieth gray" seemed palpable. All I could do was "lean." I didn't have anything to say—it had all been said. I didn't need to say it again. So I just "leaned" on Him. He didn't say anything either. He was just there. I felt strength, perspective, and peace flowing into me, enabling me for the day ahead. One day at a time!

###  Until the Storm Passes

*From Paul, March 03, 2002*

Rebecca and I have regained our equilibrium. We were both destabilized by last week's happenings—but He carried us through the pain and confusion to a settled place of peace again. Psalm 119: 92 says, "If your law had not been my delight, I would have perished in my affliction" (NIV).

*Thomas Merton says that "Providence is God's love worked out each day." Surely You, Lord, are my Providence unfolding.*

When life is swirling out of control (and I've learned that control is an illusion, indulged in by the strong; the weak know it to be a mirage) one must "do the next thing," and try to do it His way until the storm passes. In Philippians 4: 8, Father, through Paul, tells us things on which to meditate: that which is true, noble, right, pure, lovely, admirable, excellent, and praiseworthy. There are lots of things on which one can let one's mind linger, but they are not all redemptive and helpful. What a struggle it was last week to keep our thoughts where He wanted them. When we were unable to, we began to "perish in our affliction." His grace proved strong in our weakness. That has now passed. George MacDonald says: "Minutes and hours outrun even the darkest of days." Amen!

Life can change so quickly; it is like a kaleidoscope. Sometimes we go from planned event to planned event, with ordered transitions. At other times unwanted disastrous events are cast upon us by Providence. The only way to remain at rest is to fix our eyes on You. Thomas Merton says that Providence is God's love worked out each day. Surely You, Lord, are my Providence unfolding.

There is such a tiny slice of reality that is mine—so limited I am by time and space. And that little slice is all I have. Merton said, "The sacrament of the present moment" is all that is mine to give to You. And it is only here, in this moment enshrined, that I can find You.

I only lose when I determine, or endeavor, to control my reality by judging and choosing with my puny opinion what I want or what is best for me. Help me, Lord, to leave my days and times in Your good hand. You are turning our kaleidoscope, and, as You turn, great grace will surely flow.

## DURING REHAB

At Pellenburg Rehabilitation Center after the time in ICU and Hospital, March 27, 2002 – April 11, 2003

 ### Playing with the Cards We've Been Dealt

*From Paul, while Rebecca was in Rehab*

I remember one of the insights I had after Rebecca's accident: I must "play the game" with the cards I am dealt, whether I like them or not. Of course, the thought came with the deep sense of kind Providence—that we have a Father who loves us, is committed to us, and is overseeing our circumstances. We can trust Him! The reality that the hand dealt us isn't the one we wanted, (and may not be a winning hand), doesn't abrogate the reality of Father's sovereignty. He just has a different idea than we have, and probably different goals.

He has plans that are at times mysterious, but we have confidence that He works all things into His plan for good. This gives a security in the midst of upheaval. It also gives us the confidence to go forward, to 'do the next thing,' with an underlying trust in Him.

This may not, immediately at least, change the circumstances or the emotions about them. It does provide access to the peace He said He'd give and the joy (His own) that comes to us from outside our circumstances. I'm incredibly grateful that Father commanded us to keep our focus fixed on Jesus: mind, heart, and eyes. He is our principal reality, and we see all things in the light of His face and His presence. He Himself is the primary impact on us. Our circumstances make only a secondary impact. We see all our circumstances through Him and in the light of Him. What a gift the Father gave us in Jesus and in the command to keep Him the highest, deepest, most central reality in life.

##  New Beginnings

On Friday afternoons, at 2 o'clock, I have a new handwriting class. This past Friday, I made my first entry into my journal. It is scrawling but readable. Surely it will only get better.

And at mealtimes we put a pillow and towel on my lap, (the towel covers all my upper body). I have begun to eat by myself. Now, I am not ready for fine dining just yet, since I'm eating only with my fingers. Occasionally I use a fork to spear something, but it can get messy. Like the writing, though, it is a good first step. Beginnings are often difficult but as we overcome the result is such peace and joy in accomplishment and new life.

## His Life Springing Up

There is a deep life in me that makes each part of the journey a joyful spring. I am ever reminded of Psalm 84:6: "As they pass through the valley of Baca (weeping) they make it a place of springs" (NIV).

I am so aware that whatever people see in me does not come from me and so it must be His life, springing up.

## AT HOME

Home to stay, April 11, 2003

 **Peace That Comes Through Relationships**

Many times throughout this journey, 24-hour days of prayer have been launched on my behalf. I saw myself as the paralytic with my friends carrying me to Jesus and lowering me on the mat of their love and prayers.

I think this was especially significant in the week of transition from being in the hospital to being at home. It was a bit wrenching to leave Pellenberg. I had been there for so long, in the security of nurses and doctors. This week has been the beginning of working with our new "team," a nurse who comes twice a day and a physiotherapist who comes once a day. The physiotherapist is excellent and working me hard. Of course, it is such a joy to be awakened every morning by my beloved Paul and surrounded by my family and friends. Annie is here with us for a month, and that is always a delight.

Who, at 58, has the opportunity to start over? God is so good, and I am blessed by the prayers and support of so many. When I consider Father's plan, I stand in amazement. When I fell two years ago, He looked through time and saw the network of friends and family that He would weave together into a pattern for my good.

*From Paul, April 17, 2003*

I want to continue Rebecca's last thought concerning the first evening of her homecoming. Kneeling by her bed, I said to her, "This is the first day of the rest of our lives." We're together starting a new phase of life, under the careful oversight of the Lover of our souls. We stand with expectation to see what He will do.

 **One Day at a Time**

I think it was significant to have special prayer during my first week at home. You can imagine that, as thrilled as I am to be here, the week was one of great adjustment. For two years I only had to press a button for any care that I might need. One of my hardest moments was the morning I awakened feeling an overwhelming sense of my limitation and the pain of the reality that my need for constant care must be a burden to my family and friends. When Paul came back down for breakfast after our individual devotional times, I began to cry, saying, "I can't imagine spending the rest of my life like this. How can I do this?" He listened to me and then quietly said, "One day at a time!" Such a load lifted from me, because that's what Father has promised, grace for one moment at a time. Since then, there has been a joy in awakening in His presence, wondering what He has planned for that day.

Many months later, on another afternoon while Mieka was visiting, I

> *I asked Mieka what happens to someone in my situation. "I'm an invalid and in diapers," I said. I'll never forget this. Mieka looked at me and said, "Rebecca, you only have to be concerned about today. You only have one day at a time."*

asked her, as a medical friend, what happens to someone in my situation? "I'm an invalid and in diapers," I said. I'll never forget this. Mieka looked at me and said, "Rebecca, you only have to be concerned about today. You only have one day at a time." Some of these lessons have been hard learned and are continuing. Day by day He gives His peace and joy.

###  Available to Him

Each morning Hope, our little gray dog, runs and jumps on my bed, delighted that I'm not going anywhere—that I'm right here. This week the Lord gave me a word from Psalm 4:3, "...the Lord has set apart the godly for himself" (NIV). I think He feels the same about my being quiet before

Him as Hope feels about her being with me. I'm just available to Him in a way I've never been before—and it is rich.

I once heard a simple definition of Redeemer: "one who makes good." As I was awake last night, I prayed for many of you. I prayed that this week, whatever your situation, you would find the Redeemer. He died to make all things new, and it is His delight to do it. He longs to take our broken places and make such good of them for His Kingdom's glory and our joy.

##  Rushing Through Life

*"You must not rush through life."*
*I am afraid it was just the first of many such words spoken to me. Hebrews 4 says there is a rest for the children of God.*

*From Rebecca, January 03, 2007*

You may remember that at the New Year I always ask the Lord for His perspective and for a word for the coming year. In my Bible reading, I turned to John 15, the vine and the branches. I always get excited at this place in John, knowing the riches that lie ahead. As I began to read, I realized that this would be my perspective for 2007.

At that moment, Susannah came in to bring me something. Having a full day ahead of her, she was moving quickly (as she is often prone to do). "Susannah," I said, "go slowly, sweetheart."

She smiled and said, "Momma, you know I don't believe in doing anything slowly." I realized that is exactly how I have gone though most of my life.

I flashed back to a time when Susannah was about 6 years old. We had gotten into the car on our way to buy a pumpkin. We had planned a special outing together. She looked at me with a horrified expression on her little face. "Oh Mommy, I have to go to the bathroom. I will hurry really fast!" With that, she jumped out of the car and ran into the house. I watched her going, her little pigtails flying behind her.

I will never forget it. The Lord said to me, "You must not rush through life." I'm afraid it was just the first of many such words spoken to me. Hebrews 4 says there is a rest for the children of God. John 15:5 says, "I am the vine, you are the branches. He who abides in Me, bears much fruit; for without Me you can do nothing" (NKJV). Could it be that, forty years later, I'm beginning to rest in Him?

One of the biggest changes in me through the process of the last years is that I often find conversation difficult. My voice is not strong, so when there is a large group of people communicating in a lively manner, I can't get into the conversation. I have to be careful or I withdraw and am just quiet.

> *I saw the Lord gather the scattered branches together and tuck them securely into the Vine. In that gathering is a settledness and quietness.*

This happened to me on Christmas day around the table. My dear family was all gathered and having a wonderful time together. I was at the end of the table and began to feel insecure and isolated. I found myself withdrawing. I knew it wasn't right and it was not what they would want, but I didn't want to hinder their conversation and joy, so I smiled and, I'm afraid, withdrew.

Later I talked with Paul and Susannah about it. When I read John 15:5, I felt it resolve. I understood! Somehow in that situation, my soul got scattered. I saw a picture of the branches scattered, and then I saw the Lord gather the branches together and tuck them securely into the Vine. In that gathering I found a settledness and quietness. I could almost feel myself drawing from the Vine all that I needed for the situation. As I approach the New Year, sometimes my soul is scattered. I will gather it together into the Vine and rest in that place.

Isn't it marvelous! What Father wants of us is to be quiet, to be in faith and to draw from Him—allowing Him to "be" all that we need Him to be.

So my new word for this year is an old word with fresh life: *rest!* Let Him grant us to gather our scattered souls into Him and rest in quietness as we go about our business. ✴

CHAPTER NINE

# My True Value

"O Lord, You have searched me and known
me...You formed my inward parts...I will
praise You, for I am fearfully and
wonderfully made..."

Psalm 139:1, 13, 14 (NKJV)


"...You have relieved me in my
distress...But know that the Lord has set apart
for Himself him who is godly; The Lord will
hear when I call to Him...Meditate within
your heart on your bed, and be still.
...Lord, lift up the light of Your countenance
upon us. You have put gladness in my
heart...I will both lie down in peace,
and sleep..."

Psalm 4: 1, 3-4, 6-8 (NKJV)

WHEN THE ICU DOCTOR SAID, "IN THIS UNIT YOU are the sun," I felt like a sad-looking sun! How can that be? Visitors stood around my bed, where I lay surrounded by tubes, wires, and bandages, covered only with a sheet. We laughed and talked, but I was only able to whisper. Sometimes they had to read my lips.

At that time we had a good friend who came to visit. He laughed and said I talked more than anyone he'd ever been with who couldn't speak. They went away encouraged and strengthened, saying how much they enjoyed their visit. The more this happened throughout the months, I began to be in wonder. It was confusing. What was happening? It wasn't how I looked (I'd always been careful about my weight, my hair, and my make-up). It wasn't my brilliant conversation. It wasn't my service toward them. Could it be something of who I was and who God had made me that blessed them and that they loved?

*Paul said, "Doctor, I want her back. We'll take her however we can get her." I have begun to touch the reality that our true value is not in what we do, but in who we are.*

The greatest expression of this to me has been through my beloved Paul. The doctors told him in the beginning that I would be a vegetable, and they wanted his permission to pull the plug if there was difficulty during the surgery. He refused, saying, "Doctor, I want her back. We'll take her however we can get her." And through these years he has been there, standing with me, loving me. I believe in these years I have begun to touch the reality that our true value is not in what we do, but in who we are.

## DURING ICU AND THE HOSPITAL

Immediately after the accident, October 4, 2001 – March 27, 2002

 **"It's About My Love": Father's Fight for Me**

It is difficult for me to express the terror of those long nights, as I lay trapped in the silence of my own body. Then, in His compassion, Father sent an "angel" nurse to care for me—such an expression of His love! At that point, to many, it would have seemed that I had no value, being little more than a vegetable. But, oh, my Father valued me and in my terror sent a man to come. He reassured me all through the night that I would not be alone and that he would be close by.

> *I fear there is nothing left of me. Yet, Father is fighting for me. Somewhere deep within my soul I hear His voice.*

The realities of life now are blinding pain, inability to move, and hissing of a machine that I suppose is enabling me to breathe. And why do we bother? It seems there is such a battle swirling around. I fear there is nothing left of me. Yet, Father is fighting for me. Somehow, deep within my soul, I hear His voice, "It's about My love." Oh, Lord, surely You value me beyond what I can see.

 **The Terror of the Night**

*From Paul, November 07, 2001*

Some of the most difficult times for Rebecca have been at night. She has awakened from nightmarish dreams of being unable to move—to find the dream was a reality. She is making good progress but is still unable to do anything for herself. If there were a crisis, she is dependent and vulnerable.

These are not easy realities to process. One of the night nurses came into her room one evening, noting her anxious expression. She cannot yet push a button or call out for help. If someone isn't watching, she has no way to communicate. The nurse said: "Mrs. Petrie, I will look in every few minutes. I'm watching you, and I will take care of you." She slept well that night.

That is so much like our Father. I felt that He was saying that to her through this wonderful caregiver. "I'm watching, and I am there." That He is, and His presence makes the difference.

## DURING REHAB

At Pellenburg Rehabilitation Center after the time in ICU and Hospital, March 27, 2002 – April 11, 2003

 ### Changing Job Descriptions

When I came to rehab, I was beginning to face the realities of my life. I had been so active and busy in caring for others and sharing my life. Now I felt set aside and sad. I felt that God would no longer use me as before.

My lifeline was in the morning early when I would seek the Lord and His strength for each day. One morning as I read Psalm 40, the Lord spoke to me that He had called me to Himself. What more could I possibly want than the rest of my life spent seeking Him, always at rest? So I began to find the joy of each day in His Presence. I began to make peace with the fact that my life had changed and God had a different purpose for me.

Years ago when Paul's ministry

> *I began to find the joy of each day in His presence. I began to make peace with the fact that my life had changed and God had a different purpose for me.*

began to go in a new direction, I felt frustrated and angry. One morning I was in the car, and I remember stopping at a red light and crying out to the Lord, "You didn't call me to this! You called me to my husband, to my children. You called me to women and to Europe, but you never called me to this."

I accelerated at that red light to go on, and He spoke, simply, as God always does, "Can't I change your job description?" I was reminded once again of that morning when I read Psalm 4. He had again changed my job description. I belonged to Him and He could call me wherever and whenever He wanted.

###  My Appearance Reflected in the Mirror

It was ten o'clock in the morning and the nurse wheeled me into the vocational rehabilitation room. "Good morning, Rebecca, and how did you sleep?" It was Stephen, the director of the rehab program. He didn't say anything else but just began the normal rehab exercises to develop my small motor skills. "Take these little blocks and move them over to this little square. And then move them back." This was a typical rehab exercise.

---

*Stephen went across the room and brought a huge mirror and wheeled it in front of me. I was horror-stricken. For almost 18 months, I had never looked into a mirror.*

---

Then, without saying another word, Stephen went across the room and brought a huge mirror and wheeled it in front of me. I was horror-stricken! For almost 18 months I had never looked into a mirror. It didn't matter how I looked, I was just trying to survive. Stephen knew that it was time. Always before the fall, I had taken great care about my appearance, my hair, my nails, my weight, my clothing, and my make-up. I remember once saying during rehab that, if I couldn't do it myself, I didn't want someone else to have to do it for me. There was already so much that had to be done for me, I didn't want to add extra things, like make-up and hair. So every morning the nurses quickly combed my hair, with little fuss. I never looked, and I'm sure I looked different every day. When I looked in the mirror that day, I saw one thing that must have been the same. My hair was long, thin, and gray! With no make-up, I looked terrible. I didn't say a word. Neither did Stephen. I couldn't wait for that hour to be over so we he could take me back to my room and deposit me back in my bed. As soon as I was alone, I cried and cried.

And then I called the nurse and made an appointment with the hospital's hairdresser. The nurse said, "She's not very good." And I replied, "It doesn't matter, I've got to do something about this gray." That day I had my hair dyed blond and I put my rings on.

*All of their love combined spoke deeply to me that my value did not depend on my appearance but, rather, on some inner quality of my soul.*

I need say no more than to tell you that the next morning when I came to my physical therapy, Frank, the therapist, said, "Marilyn, we're so glad you came today!" Frank was the best. Without his therapy too, I would never be where I am today. He had the perfect balance of pushing me to my limit, while respecting my body. I remember once I was low and feeling tremendous physical weakness, and he said to the nurse who came to wheel me back to my room, "No, I would like to take her back today." As he lovingly wheeled me back down the hall, he said, "I'm afraid you're getting too tired. You need to come tomorrow for stretching, but I don't want you exercising for several days." His sensitivity and care touched me deeply.

In my weakness and lack of concern about how I looked, of course my family loved me. So did Frank and Stephen. All of their love combined spoke deeply to me that my value did not depend on my appearance but, rather, on some inner quality of my soul. In my weakness, He was strong and revealed Himself in a way that He may not be able to do when I'm strong. 2 Corinthians 12:9 tells us that His strength is made perfect in our weakness. My true value doesn't rest on my strength or how I look, or how much I weigh, but on Christ within me.

##  Pastries and Fellowship

For many years before the fall, a group of women and I would go out to a famous French restaurant, Au Vattel. We met regularly to celebrate each other's birthdays. After the accident, I was of course missing from the fellowship. One day I received a call from my friend Laura. "Since you have not been able to join us at Au Vattel, we're going to bring Au Vattel to you! So the date was set and on the given afternoon, all my friends arrived. Was it 8 or 10 of them? All I remember was the hospital staff was overwhelmed with all these talking women. As my Paul has said, "It's amazing to me that women can all talk at once and still understand each other!"

They arrived with pastries from the restaurant and Laura' entire antique teacup collection, with a lace tablecloth for my little table—all the fixings for a beautiful tea party. We laughed, ate too much pastry, and enjoyed one another. They were particularly sensitive and so it was a much shorter time than we usually spent, but long enough not to tire me.

I remember at the time I could not understand why they had come, realizing it had to be because they loved me. It was certainly not because I was giving them anything. I had nothing to give them but myself. True relationships carry through even the moments of life when we have nothing to give.

## AT HOME

Home to stay, April 11, 2003

 **Choosing Life**

*From Rebecca, December 21, 2003*

Josie (our Swedish angel who came to help) recently returned from an international gathering in London. As we sat at the dinner table on her first

> *"I will not die,*
> *but live, and will*
> *proclaim what the Lord*
> *has done."*
>
> Psalm 118:7 (NIV)

night back, she began speaking about a friend of ours there in London who talked about his recent experience. The Lord had spoken to him to choose life and not death, blessing and not cursing. Josie went on and shared about the rest of the retreat, but "choosing life" kept echoing in my mind. The next morning when Judy came down, I shared it with her. She remembered a teaching that Derek Prince had done years ago from Deuteronomy 30. We turned to it and read together, weeping. I realized that through these recent years I had never chosen life, and that God was setting life before me. It was now mine to choose. As we prayed, I chose life and blessing! The next evening, Josie and I were reading a scripture chosen randomly from my prayer quilt to read before going to bed. Psalm 118:17: "I will not die, but live, and will proclaim what the Lord has done" (NIV). I couldn't believe it! Surely the Lord was confirming my choice.

The next day I received a card from a dear friend in Lexington. In her card, she told the story of a rose. She said she had planted 3 rose bushes outside her kitchen window. She had named the white one "Rebecca." The frost came, and so she went to the window expecting to see all the roses frozen. Two of them were. But "Rebecca" was still blooming. Two more frosts later; "Rebecca" had budded and bloomed again before finally succumbing to winter's blast. She said it was so amazing that she had to write to me, because "Rebecca" just kept on living.

I had to write this to you because I feel like it is a milestone in our journey. The next week, I was invited to a friend's anniversary party. As we dressed to go out to be with people, away from the home, for the first time, I knew I was choosing life. It was difficult, and yet it was a delightful evening. The next week was the European Prayer Breakfast. We were invited to a lovely dinner party the evening before the big event. I knew I couldn't stay for the entire meal, but I did go for the hors d'ouvres. It was a most lovely evening. As I sat that evening amidst precious friends who were so blessed to have me with them again, I chose life. I knew it was a new day.

And now I'm in my new room. I have windows on two sides out to the garden ("backyard" in the USA). Our children are here to celebrate the blessed birth of our Savior together. How many opportunities each day do we have to choose life, instead of death, to choose His blessing instead of cursing!

> *"...I have set before you life and death, blessings*
> *and curses. Now choose life, so that you and*
> *your children may live and that you may love*
> *the Lord your God, listen to his voice and hold*
> *fast to him. For the Lord is your life..."*
>
> Deuteronomy 30:19-20 (NIV)

 ## New Beginnings

*From Rebecca, January 11, 2004*

I love the beginning of months: April 1$^{st}$, August 1$^{st}$, and October 1$^{st}$. I love that the Lord is giving us signposts along the way whereby we can learn "...to number our days aright, that we may gain a heart of wisdom"

(Psalm 90:12, NIV). So you can well imagine that I love the beginning of the year.

These last weeks, I've been meditating on the good things that Father will have for us in 2004. I happened to be reading in Psalm 90:4, "For a thousand years in your sight are like a day that has just gone by, or like a watch in the night" (NIV). I have long given up on New Year's resolutions. I never can seem to carry them through. But I do love to ask the Lord what He is saying to me for the coming year.

The other morning Paul walked through my room, and it came to me that I "'get to do" this thing called life with him. Suddenly it all came together in my mind. My life is incredibly brief. Paul's life is incredibly brief. And we get to live at the same time in history—together! I thought of Judy, Josie, Annie, and each of you, that in the divine purpose of God we are all here in this brief 'wink of an eye' at the same time to share the great adventure called life, in Him.

I've thought about this truth each day since. I hope it will stay with me through this year, that we will finish our task together, completing His purpose for us, and seeing what He will do this year—this "wink of an eye." Thank you so much for standing with and praying for us. "The future is as bright as the promises of God."

Note: The following year Josie was married to our third child, Phillip. What a joy to see them together finding the good purpose of God in their own lives. �֍

CHAPTER TEN

# Strength in Weakness

"...My grace is sufficient for you, for my power
is made perfect in weakness."

2 Corinthians 12:9 (NIV)


"For to be sure, he was crucified in weakness,
yet he lives by God's power.
Likewise, we are weak in him, yet by God's
power we will live with him to serve you."

2 Corinthians 13:4 (NIV)

WHAT DOES THE APOSTLE PAUL MEAN WHEN HE says, "...My strength is made perfect in weakness"? Through the years I have pondered these words over and over. I am still not sure what they mean. I have found this introduction difficult to write. There are so many examples that flood to mind. This entire story has been one of impossibility. I am so weak, so often, when life demands strength. Where does it come from?

Physical therapy is one example of the many moments when I do not have the strength to do what is required. How often have I cried out, "Lord, I can't do this; only You can do it." Elizabeth Elliot speaks of "doing the next thing." And so I would begin to do the next thing—and the task would be accomplished. Often it would leave me in complete exhaustion. But there are other examples where strength upon strength has been mine, leaving me full of joy in the end.

*Where does the strength come? In Colossians 1:27, Paul says, "...Christ in you, the hope of glory." He is in me, and when I am weak, I cry out for His grace.*

I think so often of situations even now. Paul and I have plans to go out to lunch. By the time I'm dressed, have my makeup on, and am in my chair, I feel so weary and weak. I say to my caregivers "Pray for me—I don't think I can do it." It has come to be a joke among us, because I sometimes come home so full of strength and joy that I don't want to go back to bed, wanting rather to stay longer in my chair and go out to sit on the deck.

From where does the strength come? In Colossians 1:27, Paul says, "...Christ in you, the hope of glory" (NKJV). He is in me, and when I am weak—so very weak—I turn to Him, I cry out for His grace, "Lord, I can only do this if You enable me." He is delighted, He can prove Himself, He can show Himself, He can be in me what only He can be. He can be His strength in my weakness.

## DURING ICU AND THE HOSPITAL
Immediately after the accident, October 4, 2001 – March 27, 2002

 ### Out of My Weakness

The apostle Paul says that, in our weakness, His strength is made perfect. Surely I have never been weaker. I cannot say that I see strength being made perfect, but I am amazed that when people come to see me, they seem to be deeply touched, even though I cannot speak with them.

*I am amazed that when people come to see me, they seem to be deeply touched, even though I cannot speak with them.*

I realized this week that it must be Him. I had another example this week when the woman who cleans my room wanted to come and talk to us about praying for us, because she said we are special to her. How strange! Why would we be special to her? Once again, it must be His strength in our weakness.

 ### At Home in Him

*From Paul, February 16, 2002*

For me, seeing Rebecca's daily suffering, accompanied by her courage, is heartbreaking, and taking its toll. I am faced daily with weariness, elevated blood pressure, and an undoable "do list."

I'm reading Brennan Manning's book, "Ruthless Trust." In the last chapter he writes: "'Abba, Father,' he said, 'everything is possible for you. Take this cup from me. Yet not what I will, but what you will'" (Mark 14:36, NIV). Jesus' death on Calvary is His greatest act of trust in His Father. Jesus plunges into the darkness of death, not knowing what lies on the other side, confident only that somehow His Abba will vindicate Him. Jesus' voluntary disengagement from life is His supreme expression of persevering trust—and His blessed, obstinate, importunate trust ravishes the heart of His Abba. I think trust must somehow be a gift. It feels that way to us. And it is firm amid the swirl of our present realities.

Jesus said: "Make your home in me, just as I do in you" (John 15, The Message). I'm staying "home" these days. Life is only found in Him. He is our souls' strength and shield, our hiding place. I know that this season, too, will pass. No pain is eternal—only joy in His presence is forever.

## DURING REHAB
At Pellenburg Rehabilitation Center after the time in ICU and Hospital,
March 27, 2002 – April 11, 2003

 ## The Golden Cord

Last week I had a very black day. I kept crying, couldn't remember what I was doing, or who I was. By evening, when Paul arrived, I started to share with him and, of course, began to cry again. I cried and cried, and suddenly realized he wasn't saying anything. I opened my eyes to see him sitting beside

---

*I cried and cried, and suddenly realized Paul wasn't saying anything. I opened my eyes to see him sitting beside me, weeping. Why is it so healing to have someone weep with you?*

---

me, weeping. Why is it so healing to have someone weep with you? We just held each other and cried. There was no need to speak a word. I could feel the load and the heaviness lifting. What power there is in two people of one accord standing together in Christ!

I finally said, "I just need once again to get hold of a thread."

Amy Carmichael called it the "golden cord." What was my "golden cord" back to the heart of God? Then I remembered that God is good, and that many were praying for me. I knew that, because of His goodness, I didn't have to do anything. I could just cast myself on the strength of their prayers, and rest there until He helped me. I was peaceful the rest of the evening. And the next morning I awakened in His presence.

> *I even did my first email during therapy on Friday...with an apparatus strapped to my elbow, giving me the ability to punch the keys with one finger.*

I finished the week with good faith, good strength, and courage in place of weakness. I even did my first e-mail on the computer during therapy on Friday. Now this is with an apparatus strapped to my elbow, giving me the ability to punch the keys with one finger—but it worked. And I must say, it was great fun. I could tell that Stephen, my therapist, was proud of me, and happy. It was a long way from the tears of the night before.

 ## More and More Progress

*From Paul, October 17, 2002*

Rebecca is driving her new wheelchair with ease and confidence—even going in and out of elevators. Her nausea has substantially lessened, allowing her more extended times of therapy. We pray that it will not again become a limiting cause. She has extended her time sitting up in her chair to 1 hour and 20 minutes at a stretch. Today, for the first time, she used an exercise machine, kind of like the wheel of a bike, for the strengthening of her legs (her right leg is still quite weak).

Also, yesterday the doctors stopped the night feeding through the stomach peg. She is now eating enough on her own to sustain herself. These are all answers to prayer. The progress is "little by little," but progress nonetheless, and we are grateful.

**Climbing Mount Everest**

*Then my mind went to Psalm 23:1,4-6 (NIV), "The Lord is my Shepherd, I shall not be in want. Even though I walk through the valley of the shadow of death... You prepare a table before me... Surely, goodness and love will follow me all the days of my life..." I found myself strengthened by His Word...*

This has been a difficult week. Whoever said that rehab was like climbing Mount Everest was right. Obviously, I've never climbed Mount Everest, but it can't be more demanding than this. For example, I sat yesterday between the bicycle and the exercise bench waiting for my therapist. After my therapy sessions, I returned to my room nauseated and with dry heaves from exhaustion. The experience was so traumatic, I wondered if I would faint or throw up before the therapist arrives tomorrow!

Then my eyes fell on the meadow outside the window and the hillside beyond. It was a beautiful setting, with spring coming everywhere. I thought of Psalm 121:1-2, "I lift my eyes to the hills—where does my help come from? My help comes from the Lord, the maker of heaven and earth" (NIV). Then my mind went to Psalm 23:1,4-6, "The Lord is my Shepherd, I shall not be in want. Even though I walk through the valley of the shadow of death... You prepare a table before me... Surely, goodness and love will follow me all the days of my life..." (NIV). I found myself strengthened by His Word and when it was my turn for therapy I was able, with His strength, to go on. Then we had lunch—a table prepared before me! Daily He strengthens me in my weakness.

##  Strength: Enduring the Unendurable

*From Paul, April 14, 2002*

I want to quote a compilation of verses on strength from *The Message*:

*"Our Lord is great, with limitless strength...*
*I was given the gift of a handicap to keep me*
*in constant touch with my limitations... I*
*begged God to remove it... Then He told me:*
*'My grace is enough; it's all you need. My*
*strength comes into its own in your weakness.'*
*Once I heard that... I quit focusing on the*
*handicap and began appreciating the gift. It*
*was a case of Christ's strength moving in on*
*my weakness. Now I take limitations in*
*stride, and with good cheer... abuse, accidents,*
*opposition, bad breaks. I just let Christ take*
*over. And so the weaker I get, the stronger I*
*become... It is strength that endures the unen-*
*durable and spills over into joy...."*

Psalm 147, 2 Corinthians 12, Colossians 1

Rebecca, and I, need this strength in weakness—and He has promised it.

##  The Fountains of Rome

*From Paul, November 25, 2002*

Yesterday we had a mini-milestone. When Rebecca was put in her wheelchair she said, for the first time, that it felt good to be up. That may seem small, but it is a significant step. Some background: When a patient has been immobile and prone for long periods (and Rebecca was five and a half months in ICU, in addition to the subsequent hospitalization) the blood vessels lose their elasticity and are not able to keep blood in the upper parts of the body; this, in addition to metabolic changes, makes sitting up most difficult. In Rebecca's case this results in nausea, among other things. So, for sitting up to feel good, even for the first few moments, is a long way from where she has been in months past.

*One of Rebecca's nurses said, in some amazement: "You know, Rebecca, you are stronger lying in that bed than I am standing here!"*

This week we've had the joy of a visit from our friends, Timothy and Sharon Henry, and their son, Peter. While in university, Sharon spent time studying in Rome. She told us of the Roman love for fountains—the city is full of them, many dating back to the time of Christ and before. In that era there were, of course, no motors or pumps. To provide the pressure, they built the aqueducts high above the city. The water plunged down from above, forcing it into plumes in the fountains.

Last week one of Rebecca's nurses said, in some amazement: "You know, Rebecca, you are stronger lying in that bed than I am standing here." A remarkable observation! Rebecca shared with her that she had a source of strength outside herself, coming from her relationship with Jesus. Jesus said, "He who believes in Me, as the Scripture has said, out of his heart will flow rivers of living water" ( John 7:38, NKJV). Our strength comes from higher up.

We pray the spiritual strength that flows into Rebecca will strengthen her physical body as well. May His strength be yours this week.

## LONDON SURGERIES

The London surgeries took place during the time in rehab, July 11, 2002 – August 2, 2002

 **Another Setback or a Marvelous Provision of God!**

This week, before my surgeries in London, the Lord gave me Exodus 23:20 from one of my wonderful cards: "I am sending my Angel ahead of you to guard you...to lead you to the place that I've prepared" (The Message). What a comfort it is to know that He goes ahead of us, preparing our way.

We were holding steady, and fixing our eyes on the One who called us. It was decided that I needed another operation. Before the surgery, I had to lie still for 10 days. All of this came about through a series of x-rays in which they discovered that my head was not securely fas-

> *"I am sending my angel ahead of you to guard you...to lead you to the place I've prepared."*
>
> Exodus 23:20 (The Message)

tened. In the second surgery immediately after my fall, the screws that were used had not held. Thus a special surgery was now needed. And this special surgical procedure could only be done by two specialists in the world. One happened to be in London.

That weekend, our doctor was attending a conference of leading neurosurgeons from all over Europe. Because of the nature of my case, it had been assigned priority consideration. It is astounding that all these neurosurgeons were together just at this time and in this place. It was surely a divine appointment. Later, Dr. Crockard, the surgeon in London, successfully performed a very delicate surgery through my mouth.

There was a second surgery, five days later, to complete the procedure.

It was done through the back of my neck, directly at the brain stem to the second vertebrae that had been broken. The chance of survival through these two surgeries was less than 50%, but without them I would not have lived.

When I returned to rehab several weeks later one of my nurses came directly into my room. She sat on my bed and said, "Mrs. Petrie, I'm so glad to see you. I must tell you that I never thought I would see you again!" The Lord continued to show Himself able to do by His strength what was impossible by my own.

## AT HOME

Home to stay, April 11, 2003

 **Our Expectation is From You**

*From Rebecca, July 31, 2003*

When we first started writing e-mail updates, Paul and I determined that we wanted to be candid about the challenges and our responses to them. We wanted to express the reality of our day by day happenings, both in our circumstances and in our souls. Today I am discouraged. I am better than I was earlier this morning, and will be better by this evening, I'm sure. I had a good cry with Judy, or should I say we had a good cry together. I also had a good time with the Lord, so my perspective is adjusted.

I especially want to share these thoughts with those of you who have serious or extended illness. Yesterday and today I have felt that I am a terrible burden to everyone around me. The reality is that everything I need must be brought to me or done for me. Often I don't even express the things I want because there are so many. To "want" something only adds more of a burden to those who love me and are committed to my care. Everyone around me needs a break to get away. I know it is not a break from me, but a break from the burden of my constant care.

Judy expressed it well this morning when she said: "He is faithful to bring us all to a place where we know we need Him. We can't do it on our own." She, in her extremity and weariness, sometimes not knowing if she can go on, and me in my inability to bear being so needy, wanting to get up and do something for myself. The Lord has to teach us how to do this.

All along my cry has been: "Lord, teach me, show me. I don't know how to do this. Teach me how to go through the day as You would." It is in our extremity that we truly find Him. He brings us through phases, doesn't He? We go along and then He takes us to another level. This morning the Lord led me to Psalm 62: 5-8 and 11-12 (NIV):

*"Find rest, O my soul, in God alone;*
*My home comes from him.*
*He alone is my rock and my salvation;*
*He is my fortress, I will not be shaken.*
*My salvation and my honor depend on God;*
*He is my mighty rock, my refuge. Trust in him*
*At all times, O people;*
*Pour out your hearts to him,*
*For God is our refuge.*
*One thing God has spoken,*
*Two things have I heard;*
*That you, O God, are strong,*
*And that you, O Lord, are loving...."*

Lord, our expectation is from You. We look to You and know that even through days like these, You'll bring us into a wide place.

## ✤ Silence at the Dinner Table

I find myself now in a different role than I was before. Sometimes I'm still frustrated at the dinner table as lively conversation proceeds—our family has always been vivacious and talkative, and sometimes I am unable to get a word in edgewise. Now Paul and Susannah try to be sensitive and when they see me struggling, they often stop the conversation and give me the opportunity to speak. Sometimes I sit and talk with the Lord and He reminds me that it's OK not to talk and just to be quiet. My weakness, once again, is made perfect in His strength.

##  Choosing the Things That He Chooses

*From Rebecca, June 07, 2004*

Several weeks ago, I was in a discussion with Donatienne, my physical therapist. She mentioned that quadriplegic and tetraplegic are the same thing, just in two different languages. She had always said that I was a tetraplegic. I thought this was a term meaning that I was only paralyzed in three limbs, since I could use my left arm. "Oh, no," she said. "You only have partial use of your left hand and arm and are considered a quadriplegic." This was hard for me.

> *"Lord, change my mind, and teach me what is good."*

I had not seen myself as a quadriplegic. It was difficult for me even to say it. About a week later, I was talking to Susannah on the telephone and I shared it with her. I began to cry. She said, "Mother, there is something wrong with the way you're thinking." She went on to tell me that very week she had been reading in 1 Corinthians 1:27 where Paul says the Lord chooses the weak things. She realized that she didn't choose the weak things. She chose strong things. And she cried out to the Lord that He would enable her to choose the same things that He chooses. I said that it reminded me of when I said to the Lord, "Change my mind, and teach me what is good." "Yes, Mother! Ask the Lord to let you see it as He sees it."

The next morning I turned to 1 Corinthians myself. At the top of the page in the second chapter I had written, "Change my mind, and teach me what is good." It was while reading this very passage the Lord had begun to speak these truths to me. I also turned to Romans 12:1-2 where Paul expressed the same ideas.

> *"Therefore, I urge you brothers, in view of*
> *God's mercy, to offer your bodies as living*
> *sacrifices, holy and pleasing to God—this is*
> *your spiritual act of worship. Do not conform*
> *any longer to the pattern of this world, but be*
> *transformed by the renewing of your mind.*
> *Then you will be able to test and approve*
> *what God's will is—his good, pleasing,*
> *and perfect will."*
>
> Romans 12:1-2 (NIV)

So I've been making this my prayer these last weeks and I'm much further along in accepting, at yet another level, what has happened to us. It is a wonderful thing that the Lord wants to get hold of our minds and change them, so even our thoughts are in conformity with His thoughts, enabling us to choose the things that He chooses. As we allow Him to change our minds and give us His thoughts and perspective, we prove how good His will is.

##  His Poem

*From Rebecca, March 9, 2007*

"For we are His workmanship [which could be rendered as 'His poem'], created in Christ Jesus for good works, which God prepared beforehand that we should walk in them" (Ephesians 2:10, NKJV). When I read this verse this week, my heart leaped. I have normally focused on the first part, rejoicing that I was "His poem." But this time, I saw "...good works, which God prepared *beforehand...*" He has gone ahead of me in all that He calls me to do.

I remembered an experience that I had when I was in Intensive Care. I had had an examination that was extremely painful. Afterwards, to my horror, they said they had to repeat the process. As I faced the second procedure, I was frightened and filled with dread. While waiting for the second exam, I glanced over my left shoulder and became aware of Jesus' presence. He was young and strong. As I watched in this "vision," the doctor did the same procedure on Him. He looked over at me and said, "I will always go before you."

We have been blessed to see this same reality working out in the lives of our children. Our Susannah is starting a new part-time job and as I prayed for her in this new state of affairs, I realized the Lord Jesus had "works which He had prepared beforehand" for her to do in that place. He had prepared them long ago; all she has to do is walk where He has gone before.

Often, when I go out for an appointment or outing, I feel anxious. I am afraid I won't have the strength to do what will be required. But, every time it goes well and I have all that I need. Every time He goes before me, preparing where I should roll. What a delightful confidence we have in Him who is revealing Himself to a lost world through our "good works."

CHAPTER ELEVEN

# *Power of Prayer*

*"...I say to you, whatever you ask the Father
in My name He will give you. Until now
you have asked nothing in My name. Ask, and
you will receive, that your joy may be full."*

John 16:23-24 (NKJV)

THERE IS A CLINICAL STUDY OF THE MOLECULAR structure of people who are ill. The theory is that some people have bodies that have a molecular structure that lends itself to healing and recovery. The gentleman who talked to Susannah about this program asked if her mother would be interested in participating. What an interesting concept! What happens when we pray? As I write this, it will be five years in October since I fell. It has been 5 years of being soaked in the prayers of faithful people. Could the Lord, through the prayers if His people, be changing my molecular structure?

Sometimes we receive e-mails expressing almost disappointment that I'm not walking. But my continued progress is unprecedented— unexplainable. I feel there might be things in life better than walking. I feel so very privileged to be the constant recipient of the prayers of those who love me. And God is faithful: working, working—always working. As we pray with thanksgiving, our confidence is not in what we see, but in the One who is faithful. In these next vignettes, you will see time after time when the prayers of Father's people carried me through and made the difference.

## DURING ICU AND THE HOSPITAL
Immediately after the accident, October 4, 2001 – March 27, 2002

 **Leaning into Prayer**

*From Paul, October 31, 2001*

Recently, I heard a story that encouraged me. A father, with naval background, took his son to a harbor. There was a large ship docked next to the pier. The father said: "I can move that ship." He planted his feet on the edge of the pier, put his hands on the hull, and leaned into the boat. After 10 minutes there had been no movement. After 15, the son was embarrassed

---

*The father said, "I can move that ship." He planted his feet on the edge of the pier, put his hands on the hull, and leaned into the boat..."*

---

and wanted to leave. After 20 minutes the boat began to move. The principal of inertia was at work. If you lean into something long enough, it will move. Another friend said that things began to move at the molecular level the moment he leaned into the boat. It reminded me that we "leaned into" Rebecca's circumstances for 12 days before we started to see movement. Then her physical situation began to change. As we continue to "lean into" prayer for progress, we'll see more and more restoration. Thank you for "leaning into" Rebecca's recovery with us.

## Covered in Prayer
*From Rebecca, January 5, 2002*

These prayers have been my blanket of covering. Once, early in the morning, I had to go for what they said would be a painful examination. It was cold, and as I left the room, the nurse threw my prayer quilt over me. "You'll need this; it's cold out there this morning," she said. I lay in the hospital corridor, waiting. I felt lonely and fearful. I managed to pull the quilt up a little, and as much as I was able, I snuggled up under it. Suddenly it swept over me, "I'm covered with the prayers of Your people." I knew many were praying, and all was peaceful.

## Resting on Your Prayers

*From Paul, January 23, 2002*

Whew! Have you ever tried taking dictation by reading lips? We're learning many new skills. Here's From Rebecca,

I'm amazed that so many have stood with us for such a long time. Often I say to the Lord, "I don't have anything, but I rest on the prayers of my friends and family." *Thank you* seems so inadequate. Maybe we are finding something new in the meaning of the Body of Christ. Surely a part of my strength these days is because the Lord's people continue to stand with me.

## DURING REHAB

At Pellenburg Rehabilitation Center after the time in ICU and Hospital, March 27, 2002 – April 11, 2003

 ## "Honey, You Better Get a Bucket!"

A young physical therapy aide strapped me to the tilt board. She began to slowly tilt me. This is a process of training the body to readjust from a prone to an upright position. It's extremely difficult and painful, as the blood vessels had been only pumping the blood in a prone position, in my case for almost a year a half. Since it was her beginning days as a trainee, my

*She strapped me to the tilt board and slowly began to tilt me. But since it was her beginning day as a trainee, my young friend tilted me a little too fast.*

young friend tilted me a little too fast. As she got me up in front of the entire rehab exercise room full of my fellow patients, I began to heave. "Oh, no," she cried, "You can't do this. It's my first day!" I laughed and said, "Honey, I'm sorry, first day or not, you'd better get a bucket!"

In circumstances such as mine, many things that we take for granted become great learning processes. Time and again I cried out, "Oh, Lord, let your people be praying." Often we sent out special requests for urgent needs. Many days, as I lay my head back, I would say, "Father, I can do nothing. I'm resting on the prayers of Your people." And time and again, they carried me through. Time and again we proved the power of prayer together.

 ## Carried in Prayer

*From Paul, June 14, 2002*

These are the days of preparation for Rebecca's surgery in London. Rebecca is holding steady—continuing to release herself, her life, and her future, into His hands. Earlier this week, one of her nurses asked her if she was afraid. It surprised her; she had been sad, but had not thought about being afraid. Her comment to a friend, later that day was: "How's that for being carried in prayer!" Her peace and evenness are a miracle.

## DURING LONDON SURGERIES

The London surgeries took place during the time in rehab, July 11, 2002 – August 2, 2002

 ## Carried through My Surgery in London

Several weeks ago, someone said to me that I would be carried all the way through the time in London. That day I received a card from a friend with the verse: "...Let the beloved of the Lord rest secure in him, for he shields him all day long, and the one the Lord loves rests between his shoulders" (Deuteronomy 33:12, NIV). When I read the verse, I knew it was from the Lord, but I was surprised that He was carrying me between His shoulders. Then another friend sent me a card with the most wonderful picture of a lamb. When I saw it I wept, because I knew I was the Lord's lamb. I remembered the shepherd carries his lambs around his shoulders. So I went with that verse to the University Hospital, Leuven, to get my halo—a temporary device used to hold my head in place for the trip to London. When they brought the halo for us to see, the whole halter part, made of hard plastic, was lined with sheep's wool.

> *"Let the beloved of the Lord rest secure in him, for he shields him all day long, and the one the Lord loves rests between his shoulders."*
>
> Deuteronomy 33:12 (NIV)

And now here I am. The angels have gone before and I am in a lovely room in a beautiful, old hospital. There is a little balcony where wild flowers grow and pigeons come. The room is peach, blue, and cream. It is silly, but the Lord knows that pigeons, blue, and kind people mean so much to me.

The staff is the most international I have ever seen. The other day nurses from the Philippines, Nigeria, Australia, New Zealand, and England all helped with my care. They were all kind and efficient, working so well together. Truly the Lord is covering me with His love and with prayer.

I don't know what the coming days will bring. Dr. Crockard is obviously a brilliant man, and very kind. The surgery will involve two procedures five days apart. The first will go through my mouth, the second through the back of my neck at the base of my head. Dr. Crockard is one of two surgeons in the world who is able to do these procedures. In the natural, the chances of success are slight. But I know I'm in good hands—but mostly I am in Father's hands.

## AT HOME

Home to stay, April 11, 2003

 ### In It for the Long-Haul

It's astounding to me that during these years together we have had strong consistent prayer support.

A team of friends have stood with us from the time of the first e-mail and the cry for prayer that Paul sent out. Many of their friends have joined the team along the way. This team now consists of a network that spreads around the world.

---

*It's been amazing to watch the unfolding of events that have resulted from these prayer marathons on my behalf.*

---

How exciting it has been to see the powerful affect of prayer vigils and prayer weeks! Sometimes this takes the form of different people spending a half hour in prayer. Sometimes it's a whole group effort praying around the clock. It's been amazing to watch the unfolding of events that have resulted from these prayer marathons on my behalf. Often my physical therapist will say, "This spasticity is increasing again. You need to have those friends of yours pray."

Another time, she and I made a list of what needed to happen and presented the list to the prayer team. Then we continued our work in therapy. We were amazed at the rapid progress that resulted from the increased prayers. How could I ever say what it has meant to me that so many people have been so faithful in prayer!

**Good Friends Become Good Pray-ers**

*From my sister, Judy McCullough*

Without the help of the precious women here in Belgium, Rebecca's daily care would rest on the family exclusively. [This was in the early days, before the caregivers that have helped us so much began to come help.]

Someone has been with her nearly every waking moment for the last 5 months. These dear women sacrifice to help fill the schedule each day. The friends here have become a team around Rebecca and the family. They have also become a loving, praying, and practical support to me personally. It is a joy to see the Body of Christ in such full expression! ✳

CHAPTER TWELVE

# *Joy*

*"Rejoice in the Lord always.
Again I say, rejoice!"*

Philippians 4:4 (NKJV)

*"I have told you this so that my joy may be in
you and that your joy may be complete. My
command is this: Love each other as I have
loved you. Greater love has no one that this,
that he lay down his life for his friends."*

John 15:11-13 (NIV)

JESUS SAID IN JOHN 15:11, "...THAT YOUR JOY MIGHT BE full" (NKJV). Deep in Father's heart is the root expression of joy and rejoicing. I think one of the greatest gifts my mother gave to me was laughter. She always said, "In every situation there is something to rejoice in and to laugh about."

Joy is much more than an emotion; it comes from deep within our souls. It is an expression of the life of Christ bubbling up. It's much deeper

---

*Joy is much more than an emotion; it comes from deep within our souls. It is an expression of the life of Christ bubbling up. It is much deeper than happiness.*

---

than "happiness." David, the psalmist, spoke again and again of the joy of the Lord. The New Testament is filled with references to joy being the Lord's ideal condition of our soul. And, it can be expressed in laughter.

Part of my monitoring system was a device kept on my finger at all times to track my pulse rate. One day, Susannah came in while Stephen was sitting with me. She found him with the pulsometer on his own finger. "Look, Sue, my pulse is 70!" She quickly changed it back to me, explaining to Stephen that it was an important part of my monitoring system. She then went to the nursing staff to explain the changes in my pulse that resulted from Stephen's antics.

Day after day, the Lord provided opportunities to laugh together and share the joy that often comes in the midst of pain. Laughing together lightens the load and brings a perspective that is heavenly.

# DURING ICU AND THE HOSPITAL

Immediately after the accident, October 4, 2001 – March 27, 2002

 ## Early Signs of Joy

One afternoon when Stephen was with me he began to shout, "Mama's moving her left big toe!" This was our first sign of re-enervation. What cause for celebration! The nerves were rebuilding. This was our first concrete ray of hope. After this movement, Paul, with the help of a nurse and hospital technician, designed and created a bell system that was attached to the end of my bed. I could ring for the nurse by just moving my toe. Before Paul left every evening, he made sure all was in order for me to call a nurse in the night. This monitoring device was the beginning of my "walking out." It was a turn in my struggle and growth as I learned to live my new life.

 ## Sterilizing Cell Phones

All through this journey the Lord has helped us to laugh. When we know that He loves us and He's working even in our "impossible situations," often laughter bubbles up as an expression of His abiding joy. Jesus said in John 15:11 "...that my joy will be in you and that your joy may be complete" (NIV). Once again in our extremity we prove His Word is true.

Even when I was in ICU, Stephen helped us to laugh! In my room there was a sterilizer. One day Stephen, while playing with the sterilizer, dropped Paul's cell phone into it. We were all horrified, and then we began to laugh. Somehow my family was able to fish it out and dry it out. It was none the worse for the wear. We all guessed that a sterilized cell phone was rather special.

 ## A Higher Reality

*From Paul, December 16, 2001*

Last evening when Rebecca and I were alone, she said she felt sad, being here (Room 13) at this time of year. We talked about Christmas and the joy of being with family and friends. In our conversation, we concluded that this season is not essentially beautifully decorated trees, lovely parties, and lots of gifts. There were no decorations at the manger. Father's love is the heart of Christmas.

This morning, in my quiet time I decided to read the Matthew and Luke Christmas passages again. Clearly God's intervention in Mary and Joseph's life was life changing! The anticipation of the engaged couple, of their wedding and a simple life together, was shattered! When the angel, Michael, visited Mary and then Joseph, everything changed. Their journey

*I was struck with the paradox. Two things were happening simultaneously. I have a strange contentment. Our lives seem reduced to the simplest denominator: relationships, with the Messiah and one another.*

took a different direction! Their reputation was called into question. They lived under the rule of Rome so they had to travel with Mary 9 months pregnant, from Nazareth to Bethlehem. What an uncomfortable journey! Then, there was no room! I wonder if they could they have asked, "If this is God's child, why such awful circumstances?" Then they had to flee as refugees to an unwelcoming, foreign country. This is not a pretty story!

And yet at the same time, there were angels rejoicing, "…good news of great joy that will be for all the people. Glory to God in the highest…" (Luke 2:10, 14, NIV). The Savior of all men was being born into the world.

I was struck with the paradox. Two things were happening simultaneously. I told Rebecca last evening that I have a strange contentment. Our lives seem reduced to the simplest denominator: relationships, with the Messiah and one another. We had Him—close and precious. We had one another—also close and precious. We had our wonderful family and dear, dear friends. We had His peace and a joy that makes no sense, but that is as real as Room 13 (perhaps more real). The paradox: dreadful circumstances in the natural; nothing as we would wish it to be; pain; disruption; limitation. Yet at the same time, good news; angels rejoicing; our Father's smile; our Elder Brother and Friend's companionship; great grace!

I'm grateful the higher reality is the dominant one—else we would be swallowed up in grief. As it is, He is enough, more than enough!

 ## Whatever—We'll Rejoice

*From Paul, October 17, 2001*

Next week is a critical one. Please pray the muscles in Rebecca's chest and diaphragm will work again. If she can breathe on her own within the next week, that will be a great boon to her condition, and to her prognosis—and she will be able to speak. I long to hear her voice again. Our approach is to pray through each phase of recovery as it arrives. If the Lord gives us an instantaneous healing, we'll rejoice. If it is progressive, we'll rejoice. Whatever—we'll rejoice! For now, breathing on her own is the focus. Who Rebecca is to us, and to many, does not depend on what she can do. It is *who* she is—and she is with us. For that, we rejoice.

> *"If she can breathe on her own next week, that will be a great boon to her condition... and she will be able to speak. I long to hear her voice again."*
>
> —*Paul*

 ## The Lord Has Given Joy

*From Paul, February 01, 2002*

Since the previous ENT exams have been so painful, Rebecca had questions for the doctor. "Oh, this one is simple," he said. "They'll just drop a small camera down your nose." It struck us as funny. Thank God for the ability to laugh.

One of the nurses with whom we've been sharing a lot said, "Mrs. Petrie, you and your family have brought God into this hospital." I'm sure He was here long before we arrived!

We've had increasing opportunities to share deeply with the staff here at the hospital. After 17 weeks, we're feeling like one big family.

## DURING REHAB

At Pellenburg Rehabilitation Center after the time in ICU and Hospital,
March 27, 2002 – April 11, 2003

 ### One Left Glove

"Well, I don't like to ask personal questions, but why are you wearing one brown glove?" It was the evening nurse coming into my room who noticed, for the first time, the brown knit glove on my left hand.

Upper spinal cord injuries play havoc with one's thermostat. Judy said it well the other night, "You're hot in the middle and freezing on the edges." So my left hand, which is my best hand, gets cold and stiff. Our solution: a glove for just one hand. It looks silly, but it's working well. I remember putting this same glove on both Phillip and Stephen when they were young.

 ### French Fries and Stephen

Sunday night is my special night. Our son, Stephen, comes to visit and our treat is "frites" (Belgian French fries) while we watch "Songs of Praise" and "The Antique Road Show" on the BBC. You can imagine these were not Stephen's favorite shows, but he was gracious and gladly watched them with me. What a joy it was just to be with him.

 ### Adventures in My Wheelchair

Tomorrow, Monday, I will need special prayer. My occupational therapist (also named Stephen), has been determined for some time that I would drive an electric wheelchair. For several weeks I had tried, but didn't feel secure enough to continue. My first efforts were disastrous. I ran into the cleaning man, and the walls, and barely missed several other patients. When I drove through the therapy room, I overheard someone saying he was terrified. Now, I think that was a bit extreme, but you can imagine it was a negative experience. Shortly after that time, we went to London for the surgeries—and you know the rest. Stephen now has a new wheelchair for me. I begin tomorrow. I actually feel rather excited about it.

In the days that followed, I continued and indeed overcame. I began to love my little chair and even named it the "Gracemobile." Praise God for progress and joy in new beginnings!

---

*They determined I would drive an electic wheelchair. My first efforts were disastrous. I ran into the cleaning man and the walls, and barely missed several other patients.*

---

###  Rebecca's New "Motorcycle"

*From Paul, April 28, 2002*

Rebecca got her new electrical wheelchair. She calls it her motorcycle. It is black and purple, and sleek. So far she has only run into hospital personnel and corridor walls—no other patients. Driving never was "her thing."

*A Note from Rebecca*

Today I had a near miss with the maintenance man. He jumped on his bucket with horror on his face. Another day my wheelchair malfunctioned and wheeled 'round and 'round in circles. Stephen risked his life and got it turned off. I can see why I'm so insecure about this whole process!

 ## By Hard Work, the Progress Continues

*From Annie, August 21, 2002*

It has been a busy afternoon. Physiotherapy was great today (Rebecca's words). She worked hard. Frank, the therapist, worked on both arms and shoulders. He had Rebecca hold a glass of water with the left hand and drink by herself.

> *"After some exercise, Rebecca's voice became audible several times. 'So it does work!' was her happy comment."*
>
> —*Annie*

Then the speech therapist came. Gertie worked with Rebecca on breathing and stressing the fourth word of a sequence. After some exercise, her voice became audible several times. "So it does work!" was Rebecca's happy comment.

After coming back into the room and having supper, Rebecca suddenly realized when trying to scratch her nose, that she had simultaneously moved her left arm to her face and naturally lifted her head from the pillow. She was thrilled, as it came so spontaneously.

When Stephen, the occupational therapist, came to make an appointment he was encouraging. He said that in a healthy body the nerves' healing progression is one millimeter per day. Each illness, even a cold, can freeze that process till the body is healthy again. He said that in Rebecca's case, being somewhat unique, there are still lots of things they are not yet sure about. But he was encouraged.

His short-term aim is still for Rebecca to use her left arm to feed herself, write, and drive the new electric wheelchair. The right one is to follow as much as possible. Stephen wants Rebecca to have as much independence as possible.

## AT HOME

Home to stay, April 11, 2003

 **He is So Faithful**

*From Rebecca, January 21, 2004*

I'm in my new room, and how beautiful it is. The door is automatic so I can go in and out in my electronic wheelchair (which I should have within the next month). When the door closes, there is a thump. I am alone, and I am so aware of the Lord's presence filling the room. I am filled with gratitude. His provision is so kind; my heart is full.

*"Do not worry about your life. Look at the birds of the air; they do not sow or reap or store away in barns, and yet your heavenly Father feeds them. Are you not much more valuable than they?"*

Matthew 6:25-26 (NIV)

Straight ahead of my bed is a sliding glass door out onto a wooden deck, and the garden beyond. On my left side are windows directly out into the trees. When we first moved into the house, the Lord spoke to me and said: "I have planted you in a garden." That has profound new meaning for me now.

I was reading in John 14:2 where Jesus said, "...I am going there to prepare a place for you" (NIV). It swept over me that if Paul would prepare such a beautiful room for me here, what must Jesus be preparing for us?

As I look straight out, through the glass door, I see my birds. Many of my friends have been interested in my "bird feeding." Well, be assured that we are well begun. I now have 4 feeders for the birds. They haven't found them all yet, but for those who have, it is a delight to see them flitting in to steal a sunflower seed, and flying away to eat it in the security of a high branch. I'll keep you informed as my bird feeding continues.

All of this is a constant reminder of the Lord's Word in Matthew 6:25-26, "Do not worry about your life...Look at the birds of the air; they do not sow or reap or store away in barns, and yet your heavenly Father feeds them. Are you not much more valuable then they" (NIV)? Once again, the birds are a reminder that if they are precious to Him, how much more precious are we. Often when I'm tempted to worry about silly little things, I look at my birds and I realize that He has it all in hand, and He cares for me. He cares for us. He is so faithful.

P.S. from Paul. A friend sent the following. It is, I believe, apocryphal, but the lessons are real. I thought you might enjoy reading it.

###  The Artist's Task

A concert violinist with a severe handicap came onstage and prepared to play. To see him walk across the stage one step at a time, painfully and slowly, was an unforgettable sight. He walked painfully, yet majestically, until he reached his chair. Then he sat down, slowly, put his crutches on the floor, undid the clasps on his legs, tucked one foot back and extended the other foot forward. Then he bent down and picked up the violin, put it under his chin, nodded to the conductor and proceeded to play.

> *Of course, anyone knows it is impossible to play a symphonic work with just three strings But this night, the violinist refused to acknowledge that.*

Midway through, one of the strings on his violin broke. You could hear it snap—it went off like gunfire across the room. There was no mistaking what that sound meant. There was no mistaking what he had to do.

People who were there that night thought to themselves: We figured that he would have to get up, put on the clasps again, pick up the crutches and limp his way offstage, to either find another violin or else find another string for this one. But he didn't. Instead, he waited a moment, closed his eyes and then signaled the conductor to begin again. The orchestra began, and he played from where he had left off. And he played with such passion and such power and such purity as we had never heard before.

Of course, anyone knows that it is impossible to play a symphonic work with just three strings. I know that, and you know that, but that night this violinist refused to acknowledge that. You could see him modulating, changing, and recomposing the piece in his head. At one point, it sounded like he was detuning the strings to get new sounds from them that they had never made before.

*When he finished, there was an awesome silence in the room.*

When he finished, there was an awesome silence in the room. Then people rose and cheered. There was an extraordinary outburst of applause from every corner of the auditorium. We were all on our feet, screaming and cheering; doing everything we could to show how much we appreciated what he had done. He smiled, wiped the sweat from his brow, raised his bow to quiet us, and then he said, not boastfully but in a quiet, pensive, reverent tone, "You know, sometimes it is the artist's task to find out how much music you can still make with what you have left."

What a powerful line that is. It has stayed in my mind ever since I heard it. And who knows? Perhaps that is the way of life; not just for artists, but also for all of us. So, perhaps our task in this shaky, fast-changing, bewildering world in which we live is to make music, at first with all that we have and then, when that is no longer possible, to still make music with all that we have left.

##  The Joy of Being Home

*From Paul, April 16, 2003*

This is Wednesday, April 16. Rebecca's nurse just left. We have an hour before the new physical therapist arrives, and wanted to use this time to get a note off to you all. Rebecca's transition home has been full of grace and joy.

Words are not adequate to express the delight in having her home again.

I thought her work, especially the second painting of two little birds, was great. These may seem like simple things, but since you know where Rebecca's come from, they are major accomplishments. We are so thankful for each step toward independence, however small.

*From Rebecca*

I think each morning when I wake up, it is still hard for me to realize that I'm now living at home, and not at the hospital. There were teary good-byes to my nurses, who had prepared some lovely surprises for me. As I was leaving the hospital, I was struck by the difference in my capacities now, compared to 12 months ago when I first arrived at Pellenberg. I am able to eat quite well by myself, drink from a regular glass, brush my own teeth, write legibly, hold and dial a phone, manage a remote control, turn the pages of a book, and even take my medications by myself. About three weeks ago I began again to sketch and do watercolor. It isn't what it used to be, but I wasn't discouraged with the results, and look forward to continuing this.

CHAPTER THIRTEEN

# God's Faithfulness

*"The Lord, the Lord, the compassionate and
gracious God, slow to anger,
Abounding in love and faithfulness,
maintaining love to thousands..."*

Exodus 34:6-7 (NIV)

"I CAN'T DO IT AGAIN—I WON'T DO IT AGAIN! FOR YEARS
we have had people living with us, and I can't do it again! I don't care who it
is. I won't do it." It was me speaking. We were standing in our breakfast
room. Paul was holding me. He had just suggested the possibility of a
young man moving in with us. Through the years, we'd had an "open
household." We'd had many young people live with us in a discipling kind
of relationship. Now we had moved into a "new" home. It was new to us,

and we were alone! Just Paul, our little baby, Matthew, and myself. I wanted it to be that way for the rest of our lives. I closed the doors, closed the windows, and I was quiet. *Now* Paul was suggesting a young man whom he was mentoring move into the house? I cried and let it go. Oh, God was about to prove Himself faithful. He added Kent to our family. Kent had graduated from Vanderbilt University. He was such a fine young man, and now a strong leader and a son. This was only one of the many ways that Father would prove Himself faithful to me...faithful to us. I found that God could provide, could care for my children, could bless me through my husband, and through relationships. As I let go of my own way, He would prove Himself faithful in that and many other areas time and time again.

> *The plaque hanging in my room says simply, "God is Faithful." If there is any statement that expresses Paul's and my walk through these years, it is God's Faithfulness.*

Recently, a friend in Scandinavia sent me a wall plaque, which I have hanging in my room. It says simply, "God is faithful." If there is any statement that expresses Paul's and my walk through these years, it is God's faithfulness. I've often said that His faithfulness is the framework around which our lives have been built. He called us to Himself when we were both sixteen years old. He began then to reveal Himself as one who we can trust, rest in, and know His love. Over and over again, He has proved Himself faithful.

## DURING ICU AND THE HOSPITAL
Immediately after the accident, October 4, 2001 – March 27, 2002

 ### God's Faithfulness from the Beginning

The Lord has promised to guide our steps even when we don't know to ask Him. The day we called for the ambulance, we didn't have time to seek advice for the best doctors, and the best hospital. We just went to our little, local hospital. How could we have known the Intensive Care Unit where I would spend the next seven months would be one of the best in Belgium, newly designed, with top medical personnel? It was used as an example for the entire country. I had my own private room, with glass windows for observation and the possibility for privacy and quiet. My "home" for these months was Room 13. The doctors allowed our family to be with me all through the day. It was not until nine o'clock in the evening that my beloved Paul would have to leave me. God is so faithful even when we haven't asked.

---

*"...The plans of the Lord stand firm forever, the purposes of his heart through all generations...may your unfailing love rest upon us, O Lord even as we put our hope in you."*

Psalm 33:4,11,20-22 (NIV)

---

###  "...We Put our Hope in You"

*From Paul, January 05, 2002*

These last weeks have left me with certain numbness, even fogginess. I'm beginning to get some clarity again. Psalm 33 verses 4, 11, 20-22 have been an anchor these weeks: "...he is faithful in all he does. ...the plans of the Lord stand firm forever, the purposes of his heart through all generations. We wait in hope for the Lord; He is our help and our shield. In him our hearts rejoice, for we trust in his holy name. May your unfailing love rest upon us, O Lord, even as we put our hope in you" (NIV).

These last days Rebecca has been discouraged. She said she feels that anything that can go wrong will go wrong. She is resilient, and gets hold of the

Lord. But she is also weary and worn; from the duration of this process, from the pain, from the multiple procedures she undergoes, many of which are painful, and from the process of dealing with all the loss.

We wait in hope, taking initiative in each area, with both aggressive prayer and medical attention. This is a "long obedience in the same direction" as Eugene Peterson has said. Thanks for standing-long with us. We need Him and you.

## DURING REHAB

At Pellenburg Rehabilitation Center after the time in ICU and Hospital,
March 27, 2002 – April 11, 2003

 **Baguettes for My Day**

Several months ago we received a note saying the Lord had prepared not just bread for my day, but baguettes (long loaves of French bread). In the note, my friend saw Him delivering a basket full. I do not think she realized what that meant for me, living here in Europe, where baguettes are such a part of our lives. Several days ago, a friend from London sent me a "baguette" which I have been feasting on all week. This baguette was the message in 2 Corinthians 4:16-18. 2 Corinthians is one of my favorites of Paul's letters. In it he shares so deeply of his pain and of his own heart. I have gone back and begun to reread it. Have I ever read it before? It is so fresh and alive, a "delicious baguette" for my day.

# The Way is Perfect
## Author Unknown

*Long is the way, and very steep the slope;*
*Strengthen me once again, O God of Hope.*
*Far, very far, the summit does appear;*

*But You are near, my God, but You are near.*
*And You will give me with my daily food,*
*Powers of endurance, courage, fortitude.*
*Thy way is perfect; only let that way*
*Be clear before my feet from day to day.*
*Thou art my Portion, saith my soul to Thee,*
*Oh, what a Portion is my God to me!*

## DURING LONDON SURGERIES

The London surgeries took place during the time in rehab, July 11, 2002 – August 2, 2002

 ### Faithfulness is His Nature

*From Paul, July 17, 2002*

The surgery is complete and was successful. I've spent the four hours during the operation here in her room. Friends from London offered to be with me, but I felt I wanted to be by myself with Him during this time.

Thank you for continuing to stand with us through this long season. We believed to "see the goodness of God in the land of the living." He is faithful! He can be nothing else—it is His nature.

## AT HOME

Home to stay, April 11, 2003

 ### Expressions of God's Faithfulness

*From Rebecca, October 25, 2005*

This week, we've had several lovely expressions of God's faithfulness and answers to prayer with our nurses. We've had wonderful open discussion about how a loving God could allow suffering, and how to find Him in the midst of it. What a joy it was to see our favorite nurse, her eyes brimming with tears as we touched His presence together. Another nurse, also in tears, threw her arms around me as she expressed gratitude. I was reminded of my experience in ICU. Amid the disorientation of the pain and medication, I kept hearing the Lord's voice saying: "It is all about My love."

The summer before my accident while in a church service, a man with whom I had had conflict came into the meeting. When I saw him, I felt hostility and anger rise within me. This conflict had been going on for several years, and I could not get it resolved within myself. I cried out to the Lord: "When will I be able to love him? Oh Lord, don't let him come and sit by me!" As he made his way toward me and sat down, I had to discipline myself not to move. The Lord spoke and said: "Your heart is too small." I thought: "What in the world does that mean?"

John 15:9 and 12 says, "As the Father loved Me, I also have loved you; abide in My love. This is My commandment, that you love one another as I have loved you" (NKJV). Loving one another isn't always an easy thing to do. I understand now that my heart was too small to include someone who had offended me. I had set boundaries that excluded him. They were boundaries that Jesus had not set. I believe that in these last years of suffering, many of those boundaries have been broken down, and somehow my heart seems bigger. It is a miracle! It seems that through difficulties the walls of our heart are expanded and His love is able to increase within us.

##  Opportunities for the Grace of God

*From Rebecca, February 15, 2007*

This week I'm living in Ephesians 3 (NKJV), letting the roots of my heart go deep into the richness of these words. Today as I was reading verse 7, there was a "substitution" that popped into my mind. Paul says: "...I became a minister..." And I read: "...I became a 'quadriplegic' according to the gift of the grace of God given to me by the effective working of His power." And then verse 10: "to the intent that now the manifold wisdom of God might be made known...."

I'm reading from the New King James, and my Bible highlights words and then gives Strong's Dictionary Definitions. Here it has "manifold" defined as "varied colors." "The word 'manifold' pictures God's wisdom as much varied, with many shades, tints, hues, and colorful expressions." What an incredible God we serve! Each of our situations is an opportunity for God's wisdom to be shown by the marvelous working of His grace.

Today I was sitting with Jessica, my lovely caregiver, in the waiting room of the eye doctor. We read together from Ephesians 3. I said to her: "For you, verse 7 could say, "of which I became a 'college student' according to the gift of the grace of God given to me by the effective working of His power." Each of us can identify our situations as gifts of His grace, even when the gifts may not be the one's we'd have asked for.

---

*In each of our lives there are many circumstances that must be viewed in light of His grace: a broken or difficult marriage, a child not walking with the Lord, a job that hasn't worked out.*

---

As I was working on my book, it was challenging to read again through all the early experiences after the accident and my time in intensive care. Those were days of swirling disorientation. We were not sure what God was saying or where it would end. Still, we fixed our hearts steadily on Him. Now, because of the way God has unfolded His purposes, we can see His manifold wisdom, how He has turned and used this to grow us and bless His people with events that were not what we would have chosen.

In each of our lives there are many circumstances that must be viewed in this light: a broken or difficult marriage, a child not walking with the Lord, a job that hasn't worked out. There are many scenarios in which we must hold steady and know that we will see the manifold wisdom of God expressed.

It's true for each one of us. Whatever our situation, it's an opportunity for the grace of God to show forth His wisdom. What a wonderful adventure we are on together.

##  Great is Thy Faithfulness

*From Rebecca, April 17, 2007*

I've awakened these past days singing the hymn, "Great is Thy Faithfulness." Several mornings ago, I began my quiet time reading from Isaiah. In the commentaries for chapter 2, I came to this: "Learning to abound requires never forgetting that we have been abased—and remembering that God is the only factor who has made the difference!"

As I read, I began to "remember." Paul and I have walked with the Lord for almost 45 years. As I thought about those years I reveled in God's faithfulness.

But, I also remembered great seasons of testing. Season after season we have seen relational testing followed by great lasting friendships; very difficult pregnancies followed by the joy of our two "little boys"; testing in our health always followed by increased fruitfulness and blessing. My recent accident has been a good example of this.

Then I remembered John 15:2, Jesus' picture of the Vine and the branches. "...every branch that bears fruit He prunes, that it may bear more fruit" (NKJV). I wish all of you could see the vineyards in France, and the healthy old vines there. In the autumn, the gardener comes and begins to prune. Oh no! Surely he's cut too much away! But the gardener knows what he's doing. And it is on the branch that he's pruned the new growth returns, and increased fruit is born. Where the vine is pruned, there is abundance of fruit.

We are the branches, and we belong to the Gardener. As we yield ourselves to Him, we can trust Him to direct the seasons forever increasing our blessing and fruitfulness. Great is His faithfulness! �֍

# CHAPTER FOURTEEN

# *Knowing God in the Midst of Suffering*

*"...though He was a Son, yet He learned obedience by the things which he suffered."*

Hebrews 5:8 (NKJV)

*"...that the genuineness of your faith, being much more precious than gold that perishes, though it is tested by fire, may be found to praise, honor, and glory at the revelation of Jesus Christ."*

1 Peter 1:7 (NKJV)

## The Journey's Greatest Reality

*From Paul*

I'm at my desk. Rebecca and Dorothy are working on the final draft of this book in Rebecca's room. I came to my computer to write some thoughts about God's providence. Of course Romans 8:28 is a key verse. I decided to quote from my old King James, so I pulled it off the shelf.

It is well worn with the binding failing, and is inscribed: "Presented to me by my beloved wife-to-be on February 14, 1966, the anniversary of our engagement." It is so fitting that I'd begin my thoughts quoting from her gift to me!

> *"And we know that all things work together*
> *for good to them that love God, to them who*
> *are called according to His purpose."*
>
> (Romans 8:28, KJV)

Many years ago, the Lord spoke to me that this verse was not a post-facto promise to be tacked on the end of a negative experience. It was to be the view we take towards life. This truth and this perspective have become foundational for Rebecca and me.

The story that most clearly displayed this reality for me was Joseph, Jacob's son. We know the story: the young Joseph irritating his brothers to the point of creating deep animosity toward him; the brothers taking occasion to get rid of him; his enslavement in Egypt, then in prison; his insight and revelation that open a door to rulership and a new life. Then his brothers are forced by famine to travel to Egypt to buy grain. Joseph recognizes them but they don't recognize Joseph. An emotional scene unfolds; the brothers fear for their lives. During this meeting Joseph makes one of the most remarkable statements in the Old Testament, Genesis 45: 5, 7-8 and following. I'll quote part of this.

*"...Do not be distressed and do not be angry with yourselves for selling me here, because it was to save lives that God sent me ahead of you. ...God sent me ahead of you to...save your lives by a great deliverance. So then it was not you who sent me here, but God..."*

(Genesis 45: 5, 7-8 NKJV)

It was deep in Joseph that he had gone through this life-jarring, geography-changing, painful and challenging journey in God's purpose. Father was behind it all for good! Joseph says 3 times that the deep reality, deeper than his brothers' betrayal, was the Father's wise and kind intent.

Now that's a hard one to swallow, especially if you're Joseph. But it is the deeper reality of all of our lives, and it is a foundation upon which we can stand firmly when everything in life is topsy-turvy, when agony and confusion are the strongest emotions, when nothing makes sense.

The day after Rebecca's accident, I met with our four children in our home.

We were all fractured. I said to them that it was vitally important that our present pain and disorientation not become the lens through which we viewed God. If their mother's accident became the lens, God would look distorted. It would

*"We were all fractured. I said to the children that it was vitally important that our present pain and disorientation not become the lens through which we viewed God. If their mother's accident became the lens, God would look distorted."*

be as if they were looking at me through the bottom of a coke bottle—they would hardly recognize me.

I encouraged them to hold to what they knew of our heavenly Father, and to look through Him at the circumstances—not the other way round. We had lots of questions! But our questions needed to be held before Him, not to define Him. Now, six years later, I think we know God more deeply. Here is the inscription from the Bible Rebecca gave to me on February 14, 1966:

*My Beloved,*

*There are no words...for words are such a prison. But, me, giving His Word to you is symbolic of all my life now. The three of us...one.*

*When you love someone as much as I love you, there is only one thing I can do to relieve that love...give you Him. That's why I want you to have this physical part of Him as a symbol of our love for you.*

*We are His, and not our own. He is just beginning and He is able to do exceedingly abundantly according to His power...in us (Ephesians 3:20).*

*Your wife, Rebecca*

*From Rebecca*

"You rest right here, Mrs. Petrie, and I'll be back in five minutes." The nurse left me on the hospital bed. I was completely paralyzed. All I could move were my eyes. I couldn't speak. I was waiting for one of the many tests that I would have during these early days after the fall. As I lay there right in front of me on the wall was the huge hospital clock. I watched the time. Five minutes...ten minutes...fifteen minutes...twenty minutes!!! And she still wasn't back. I was furious. Suddenly in the heat of my anger the Lord spoke, "And what was it that you had to do?" I was stricken. What had God done to me? What was the meaning of all of this?

It seems this experience marked the beginning of a great change in my soul. I'd always been a type A personality—administrative, aggressive, high achieving, always taking the initiative, and reaching the goal. Suddenly I was unable to do anything. I was not in control of any area of my life. All I could do was be acted upon. In the coming years, God worked in a deep and profound way to change the very structure of my soul. I was to go from being an aggressive Martha to a more passive Mary. As I sat at Jesus' feet in the coming years, I would learn from Him, touching His very heart. For me the change would only bring good.

*As I come to the end of this narrative, I realize once again that in the changes of life, God is always working for our good. He sees the higher good. In the crises as we look to Him and yield, He will work. ...Run to Him, into His arms and love...*

As I come to the end of this narrative, I realize once again that in the changes of life, God is always working for our good. He sees the higher good. In the crises as we look to Him and yield He will work. One, at this time, is tempted to be angry and run from Him. But if we can turn and run *to* Him, into His arms and love, He will reveal Himself and work good in our lives.

Looking back today, what a joy it is to see the goodness of God revealed in our lives. All we could do in our desperation was hold on to Him who somehow we knew loved us. Now, six years later, I see that He's given me a new life.

I have proved my relationships to be strong and good. And mostly I have proven the grace of God. He has been able to do in me what I could never do myself. He is "able to do exceedingly abundantly according to His power...in us." He is faithful! �֍

# *Appendix*

## HONOR ROLL OF CAREGIVERS

I WANT TO BE CERTAIN TO EXPRESS TO YOU, MY reader, how much my caregivers have meant to me. They are my "angels." They are literally my hands and feet. Such gifts from the Father's heart! They have all felt the call of God and I knew from the beginning that the only thing that would allow them to fulfill that call is if they loved me. So it has been my prayer that the Lord would give us love for one another. And love has been the cement of our relationships.

As we love one another, the joy of the Lord fills our home. It doesn't mean there aren't difficult moments between us—things have to be worked out—but as we come through these times, in every situation the Lord meets us. Our love and joy is expressed to everyone who comes into our home. Time and again our nurses have said, "This home is full of love. I've never been somewhere that is so happy all the time." The girls and their commitment and love are the essence of our life together. They come from everywhere, not knowing what to expect. They leave fulfilled and often wishing they could stay. Some even do return! I love each one as if they were my own. How thankful I am for each relationship. They're now scattered all over the world, fulfilling the role God has for them. Each of them has received a part of my own life. I never imagined at the time of my accident that I would have the privilege of mentoring young women for a short season of their lives. And I've had more opportunities to share Jesus with both believers and non-believers than I ever did before.

Below is a list of caregivers (alphabetized by last name); it includes those who have come for intermittent periods of time. They have been our angel support team. Those who have been present during all these years and been my backbone of support include my beloved Paul; our children, Matthew, Susannah, Phillip, and Stephen; my sister Judy McCullough (Lexington, Kentucky) who is our cook and manages our kitchen; and Annie Lisimaque (Mulhouse, France) who lives with us and carries many different responsibilities in the household. Others, like Laura Christensen, who comes every Thursday, and Monique Baja-Hamilton who comes every Monday, have continued to contribute on a regular basis, allowing the care givers a day off. There could never be enough words to say what these, and so many of you, mean to me. If I have omitted anyone, please forgive me, as the list could go on and on. I am forever grateful to the Lord for His blessing me with so many who have been there to care for me.

| CAREGIVERS | FROM |
| --- | --- |
| Rachel Adams* | Suffolk, Virginia |
| Josfine Ahlback-Petrie* | Sweden; Cleveland, Ohio |
| Wendy Beckett | Cleveland, Ohio |
| Victoria Beckham* | Fort Worth, Texas |
| Leylani Blanco* | Homestead, Florida |
| Deborah Bradfield | Atlanta, Georgia |
| Kate Byard | Dallas, Texas |
| Jessica Camenisch* | Winchester, Kentucky |
| Wade and Karen Channel | McLean, Virginia |
| Melissa Christensen | Waterloo, Belgium |

| | |
|---|---|
| Susannah Coll* | Lancaster, Ohio |
| **CAREGIVERS** | **FROM** |
| Amber Compton* | Suffolk, Virginia |
| Kristina Dalsgard* | Faroe Islands, Denmark |
| Mary Floyd | Brussels, Belgium |
| Sue Grant | Colorado Springs, Colorado |
| Sharon Henry* | Dem. Rep. Of Congo |
| Jessica Heskett* | Logan, Ohio |
| Bill and Susan Hightower | Mobile, Alabama |
| Margarett Holcomb* | Hamilton, Georgia |
| Andrew and Margaret Howell | Paris, France |
| Rebecca Joosten | Mobile, AL |
| Mary Beth Kopechek* | Columbus, Ohio |
| Anna Kopechek* | Columbus, Ohio |
| Laura Beth McCarty* | McComb, Mississippi |
| Delphine Michard | Mulhouse, France, now residing in Genval, Belgium |
| Deanna Middleton | England |
| Stacey Malholm* | Lancaster, OH |
| Anna Ostrander* | Lexington, Kentucky |
| Barbara Ostrander | Lexington, Kentucky |

(Note: Barbara has gone home to be with the Lord after a long struggle with cancer.)

| | |
|---|---|
| Diane Petrie | Toronto, Canada |
| Stephen Petrie* | Hillsdale, Michigan |
| Susannah Petrie Gjorceva* | Skopje, Macedonia |
| Debbie Piper and James | Cleveland, Ohio |
| Caroline Piper* | Cleveland, Ohio |

| CAREGIVERS | FROM |
| --- | --- |
| Sue Postle | Cleveland, Ohio |
| Sara Scaparotti | Sweden, and Cleveland, Ohio |
| Elizabeth Schenkel | Paris, France |
| Mike and Sue Shirley* | Virginia Beach, Virginia |
| Kayleigh Slaughter | Waterloo, Belgium |
| Robert and Tracey Vaughn* | Guinea, West Africa |
| Mary van Kesteren* | Brussels, Belgium |
| Abigail Walker* | Ohio |

*indicates they stayed for an extended period of several months or longer.*

Made in the USA
Lexington, KY
21 March 2010